THE NATIONAL CURRICULUM
A Critical Review

A. V. Kelly is Dean of the Faculty of Education and Professor of Curriculum Studies at Goldsmiths' College, University of London. He has written and edited numerous books and articles on education and the curriculum, including *Knowledge and Curriculum Planning*, *Microcomputers and the Curriculum*, *The Curriculum 3/e*, *Theory and Practice of Education* (with Meriel Downey), and *The Primary Curriculum*, *The Primary Curriculum in Action* and *Early Childhood Education*, all with Geva Blenkin.

THE NATIONAL CURRICULUM

A Critical Review

by

A. V. Kelly

P·C·P

Paul Chapman
Publishing Ltd

Copyright © 1990 A. V. Kelly

First published 1990

Paul Chapman Publishing Ltd
144 Liverpool Road
London N1 1LA

British Library Cataloguing in Publication Data
Kelly, A. V. (Albert Victor), *1931–*
    The National curriculum: a critical review.
    1. Great Britain. Schools. Curriculum
    I. Title
    375.00941

    ISBN 1–85396–115–9

Typeset by Inforum Typesetting, Portsmouth
Printed and bound by Butler & Tanner Ltd, Frome and London

ABCDEFG 5432109

CONTENTS

[handwritten notes at top, partially illegible]

What are your philosophies of education?

Has its implementation limited your school's education philosophies

White letter to government —

How to may individualise assessment of individual interest in accordance with N.C.

ACKNOWLEDGEMENTS

I must record my gratitude to my colleagues Gwyn Edwards and John Saxton whose comments on the first draft of this book proved most valuable in enabling me both to tighten its argument and to strengthen many of the points it endeavours to make. They must have due credit for the improvements I was subsequently able to make but no share of responsibility for any continuing deficiencies. Responsibility for these, as with the National Curriculum itself, must be accepted at source.

[handwritten notes at bottom, partially illegible]

Defining independent learning, examining different views, that would goals & purposes

(1) Historical context of Negotiable curriculum.

(2) Implications of shift of focus

(3) Examples of how schools are coping with N.C. & its' principles —

Education is what survives when what has been learnt has been forgotten.

B. F. Skinner, Education in 1984, *New Scientist*, 21 May 1964

INTRODUCTION

There are many people – and I am one of them – who disagree profoundly with the basic principles of the National Curriculum which has been introduced into all state-maintained schools in England and Wales and with its attendant structures. It is not the purpose of this book, however, merely to state and elaborate on that disagreement and dissatisfaction or to assert a contrary view. Little would be gained from such an undertaking. Rather, the intention is to reveal the details of the ideology which underpins the new policies, and to draw attention to certain internal features of them which may give cause for concern and dissatisfaction even to those who are in tune with their basic demands.

The new National Curriculum has been implemented by law for all pupils registered in state-maintained schools in England and Wales on and after September 1989. It will thus be AD 2000 before it has become fully operative and fully established, i.e. before any one year-group of pupils has experienced it in its entirety. Eleven generations of pupils will have been provided with this form of curriculum, and required by law to pursue it, before any evaluation of its effectiveness can properly be made.

This feature of educational innovation has hitherto always been regarded as a major inhibitor of educational change, and many proposed developments have in the past been criticized, and thus delayed and impeded, on the grounds that no evidence is available to evaluate in advance their merits or defects, and that children will be deprived for all time of valuable educational experience if they are the subjects of experimentation which subsequently proves to be unsatisfactory or inadequate. 'Pupil-centred' or 'child-centred' education is perhaps the best example of a proposed development which has been hampered and held back by its critics in this way, but one can cite also comprehensive secondary education and mixed-ability groupings as more recent and more specific examples of innovations which were criticized and impeded by demands for evidence of their effectiveness before such evidence could be provided.

There are, however, at least two aspects of the process of evaluation which can, and should, be undertaken in advance of implementation or prior to full implementation. Indeed, one might argue that it is irresponsible not to have undertaken these forms of evaluation before implementation of the National Curriculum was contemplated. First, while one does need to await full implementation to evaluate the effectiveness of an innovation in attaining the goals it sets itself, one does not need to delay similarly evaluation of those goals themselves. The questions of what those goals are, whether they are the right goals, whether they are the goals we feel the education system should adopt, whether there is any discrepancy between the stated goals and the required practice, and whether the goals are coherent with one another are questions which can be, and further should be, addressed and fully debated before the innovation is made.

Second, no change in education is so completely innovative that all prior research or experience is irrelevant to it. Indeed, one might argue that, if it is, it must be so idiosyncratic as to be dangerously nonsensical. Thus, with any innovation, its likely consequences, effects and, indeed, effectiveness can at least to some extent be gauged by reference to what is already known about children, about systems, about curriculum. And one can evaluate any innovation in terms of how far it has taken advantage of existing knowledge. Again, therefore, this is a form of evaluation which can, and should, be undertaken prior to implementation.

In relation to the new National Curriculum, then, both these kinds of evaluation can be undertaken now. Indeed, it can be argued with some force that both should have been undertaken before its establishment.

For the general theme of this book is that there has been a lamentable failure on the part of the planners of the National Curriculum to attempt either of these forms of evaluation or, to express it differently, to take account in their planning of any of the knowledge, the understandings and the insights which have been gleaned from the findings of many years of research, both conceptual and empirical, into educational practice and from the experience of those who have been engaged in the practice of education in many different roles and from many different perspectives.

There are two possible explanations for this failure. One is that the absence of such considerations from the planning of the National Curriculum is due to ignorance on the part of its – mostly amateur – planners of these findings and these understandings. The second is that it is due to a deliberate policy of ignoring them – both in the practical requirements of the National Curriculum and in the documentation which has been published in support of it by the

Department of Education and Science and Her Majesty's Inspectorate. Both these reasons are unacceptable and, indeed, reprehensible. The precise explanation, however, is irrelevant. What matters is that this knowledge, this experience, these understandings and these insights have not been recognized or acknowledged, and thus have not been incorporated in the plans, so that what has emerged is seriously flawed.

The planning of the National Curriculum has been conducted at three levels, and at the most crucial of these there has been little, if any, input from those with professional expertise in education. At the first level, an overall structure has been created by the politicians and their aides. Only when that structure had been established were the professionals brought in to work out the details of such things as the assessment framework and the content of individual subjects. And inevitably in undertaking that work those professionals have been seriously inhibited by the structure in which they have been required to operate. Third, the recommendations the professionals have made, even within these confines, have been referred back to those who created the original structure for modification, and that process, as we shall see in subsequent chapters, has in many cases led to a further erosion of their professional advice, so that what has emerged as required policy has not always reflected their professional input. Thus, at the two most crucial stages – that of the creation of the overall structure and that of the translation of that structure into policy for practice – there has been a disturbing failure to take proper account of professional expertise. And so, 'we have the gravely flawed product of amateurs, a hasty, shallow, simplistic sketch of a curriculum, reductionist in one direction, marginalizing in another, paying only a dismissive lip-service to the professional enterprise and initiative on which all progress depends' (O'Connor, 1987, p. 34).

It is the purpose of this book to reassert the knowledge, the experience, the understandings and the insights which reside within the expertise of those whose professional concern it has hitherto been to plan educational provision, and to hold up the National Curriculum to critical evaluation against the criteria they give rise to.

To undertake such evaluation requires a full analysis of the underlying rationale, philosophy, principles and aims of the National Curriculum, and the identification of those aspects of its practical proposals to which research evidence which is already available may be relevant. It requires an approach which is not significantly different from that of much scientific research, especially in the field of human medicine, where experimentation on human beings has long been regarded as morally unacceptable, and where the dual safeguards of appeal to all available evidence gleaned from other research sources and a clear conceptual analysis of all the moral and social implications of any proposed development have come to be regarded as a professional and ethical *sine qua non* of every practical advance.

It is a basic premise of this book that these safeguards must be, and, indeed, should already have been, applied to the experimentation which is implicit in the sweeping changes to educational provision which are required by the new National Curriculum established for every maintained school in England and Wales by the Education Reform Act 1988 and by other related provisions of that Act. The book thus sets out to apply those safeguards through undertaking the forms of evaluation described above, in order to gauge the likely impact of these new policies on the education system and, more importantly, on the individual children who are the subjects of that system.

The book is not intended, as are so many books which have appeared in the wake (an encouragingly ambiguous term) of the 1988 Act, to advise teachers and others on how to implement the National Curriculum. Rather, it is the book's concern to reveal why it is impracticable and unsatisfactory as a vehicle for education, and, if it has any advice to offer to teachers, that advice will go no further than trying to assist them to limit the damage that is likely to accompany attempts at its implementation.

1

THE NATIONAL CURRICULUM AND ITS IMPLEMENTATION

In order to undertake a critical evaluation of the National Curriculum, it is first necessary to outline in some detail what it is. This will involve not only setting out the curricular prescriptions of the Education Reform Act 1988, but, perhaps more importantly, exploring also the procedures which have been, and are being, adopted for the implementation of those prescriptions. It also necessitates a consideration of other aspects of the Act, in particular those relating to the structure, the funding and the control of the school system in the maintained sector, since these will create the context in which the National Curriculum will be established and presented to pupils. All three of these aspects of the new policies will be explored in this chapter.

First, however, it might be helpful to consider what the authors of the National Curriculum see as the rationale of their proposals and their legislation, what they state as its intentions and purposes, the reasons they offer for its introduction.

THE STATED RATIONALE OF THE NATIONAL CURRICULUM

The rationale of the National Curriculum was first adumbrated and elaborated concisely in a document published by the Department of Education and Science and the Welsh Office in July 1987. Entitled *The National Curriculum 5–16: A Consultation Document*, this publication set out in broad terms the proposed components of the National Curriculum and its associated assessment arrangements, the intended content of the planned legislation, other supportive arrangements, resource implications and the timing of the implementation of the proposals. Most important for our purposes here, however, it began by stating its rationale in terms of what it saw as the need for a national curriculum.

First, it asserted the need for 'policies for the school curriculum which will develop the potential of all pupils and equip them for the responsibilities of citizenship and for the challenges of employment in tomorrow's world' (DES, 1987, p. 2). A good curriculum, it goes on to say, will offer 'progression, continuity and coherence between its different stages' (ibid.). It assures us that 'improvements have been made' (ibid.), and that 'some standards of attainment have risen' (ibid.). 'But', it continues, 'some improvement is not enough. We must raise standards consistently, and at least as quickly as they are rising in competitor countries' (op. cit., pp. 2–3).

The declared intention, therefore, is 'to move ahead at a faster pace to ensure that this happens and to secure for all pupils in maintained schools a curriculum which equips them with the knowledge, skills and understanding that they need for adult life and employment' (op. cit., p. 3). 'Pupils should be entitled to the same opportunities wherever they go to school, and standards of attainment must be raised throughout England and Wales' (ibid.).

Such a curriculum will raise standards, the document claims, in four major ways, by:

(i)   ensuring that all pupils study a broad and balanced range of subjects throughout their compulsory schooling and do not drop too early studies which may stand them in good stead later, and which will help to develop their capacity to adapt and respond flexibly to a changing world;

(ii)   setting clear objectives for what children over the full range of ability should be able to achieve – which the pupils themselves and their teachers, supported by parents and others, can work towards with confidence. This will help schools to challenge each child to develop his or her potential . . . Far from deflating expectations, the national curriculum is intended to help teachers to set their expectations at a realistic but challenging level for each child, according to his or her ability;

(iii)   ensuring that all pupils, regardless of sex, ethnic origin and geographical location, have access to broadly the same good and relevant curriculum and programmes of study which include the key content, skills and processes which they need to learn and which ensure that the content and teaching of the various elements of the national curriculum bring out their relevance to and links with pupils' own experiences and their practical applications and continuing value to adult and working life;

(iv)   checking on progress towards those objectives and performances achieved at various stages, so that pupils can be stretched further when they are doing well and given more help when they are not.

(DES, 1987, pp. 3–4)

Furthermore, such a curriculum will:

(i)   secure that the curriculum offered in all maintained schools has sufficient in common to enable children to move from one area of the country to another with minimum disruption to their education. It will also help children's progression within and between primary and secondary education (and on to further and higher education) and will help to secure the continuity and coherence which is too often lacking in what is taught.

(ii) enable schools to be more accountable for the education they offer to their pupils, individually and collectively. The governing body, headteacher and the teachers of every school will be better able to undertake the essential process of regular evaluation because they will be able to consider their school, taking account of its particular circumstances, against the local and national picture as a whole. It will help alert teachers to problems experienced by individual children so they can be given special attention. Parents will be able to judge their children's progress against agreed national targets for attainment and will also be able to judge the effectiveness of their school. LEAs will be better placed to assess the strengths and weaknesses of the schools they maintain by considering their performance in relation to each other, and to the country at large, taking due account of relevant socio-economic factors; and the Secretaries of State will be better able to undertake a similar process nationally. Employers too will have a better idea of what a school-leaver will have studied and learnt at school, irrespective of where he or she went to school.

(op. cit., pp. 4–5)

It is this, then, that the National Curriculum is intended to do, to raise standards by offering clear statements of objectives and attainment levels, by ensuring that these represent balance and relevance to adult concerns, and by regular assessment of the levels of attainment reached, and at the same time to create the conditions for increased school and teacher accountability. To achieve this, it is claimed, such a curriculum needs the backing of law, but of 'law which provides a framework not a straitjacket' (op. cit., p. 5).

THE COMPONENTS OF THE NATIONAL CURRICULUM

The document to which we have just referred rather extensively goes on to list the components of a curriculum designed to achieve all these purposes. The Act itself divides these subjects into 'core' and 'other foundation' subjects. The 'core' subjects are mathematics, English and science, together with, in Welsh-speaking schools, Welsh. The 'other foundation' subjects are history, geography, technology, music, art and physical education, together with a modern foreign language at what is essentially secondary school level, and, in schools in Wales which are *not* Welsh-speaking, Welsh.

Merely to list subjects in this way, however, is clearly not enough. For these names in themselves mean little, and it is possible to conceive of, and to define, all these subjects in many different ways. Indeed, a feature of education in recent years has been the ways, sometimes quite dramatic, in which subjects have come to be reconceptualized by teachers and not only their content but the whole approach to them altered to match more closely what teachers have seen as the needs of their pupils. Thus 'English' has come to be known more often as 'Language', as teachers have come to concentrate on the development of the pupil's ability to use language for thinking and for talking as well as for writing, and, in the process of this change, there has been some loss of emphasis on grammatical structures, on punctuation and, in general, on the mechanics of the English language. Similar changes have wrought craft, design and technology (CDT) out of 'handicraft'. And conceptions of history as largely factual knowledge of events and their dates, and of geography as knowledge of 'capes and bays', have given way to approaches to these subjects which emphasize the development of historical, cultural, topographical, environmental and sociological understanding rather than mere knowledge.

Hence to list the subjects of the National Curriculum by name is not enough. Much more detailed definition is needed. This the Act recognizes by requiring, in section 2, that in relation to each 'core' and 'other foundation' subject there should be specified:

(a) the knowledge, skills and understanding which pupils of different abilities and maturities are expected to have by the end of each key stage (. . . 'attainment targets');

(b) the matters, skills and processes which are required to be taught to pupils of different abilities and maturities during each key stage (. . . 'programmes of study'); and

(c) the arrangements for assessing pupils at or near the end of each key stage for the purpose of ascertaining what they have achieved in relation to the attainment targets for that stage (. . . 'assessment arrangements').

Furthermore, section 4(2) of the Act provides:

The Secretary of State may by order specify in relation to each of the foundation subjects:
(a) such attainment targets;
(b) such programmes of study; and
(c) such assessment arrangements,
as he considers appropriate for that subject.

There is also an additional, negative clause, in section 5(1), that 'no course of study leading to a qualification authenticated by an outside person shall be provided for pupils of compulsory school age in any maintained school unless the qualification has been approved by the Secretary of State or by a designated body'.

Thus, to all intents and purposes, the subjects and their content which will comprise the curriculum of all maintained schools for pupils from five to sixteen have been or must be decided upon and/or approved by the Secretary of State for Education. One can see why some people call this the National*ized* Curriculum.

KEY STAGES

Reference was made above to 'key stages'. These are especially important in relation to the 'attainment targets' and the 'assessment arrangements'. For the content of each of the core and other foundation subjects is to be set out in a form which represents it as broadly divisible into four major sections, each related to a particular age group of pupils and expressed in the form of 'attainment targets' (ATs) against which all pupils are to be assessed at the end of each key stage.

These key stages are defined in section 3(3) of the Act as:

(a) the period beginning with his becoming of compulsory school age and ending at the same time as the school year in which the majority of pupils in his class attain the age of seven;

(b) the period beginning at the same time as the school year in which the majority of pupils in his class attain the age of eight and ending at the same time as the school year in which the majority of pupils in his class attain the age of eleven;

(c) the period beginning at the same time as the school year in which the majority of pupils in his class attain the age of twelve and ending at the same time as the school year in which the majority of pupils in his class attain the age of fourteen;

(d) the period beginning at the same time as the school year in which the majority of pupils in his class attain the age of fifteen and ending with the majority of pupils in his class ceasing to be of compulsory school age.

Thus the National Curriculum consists not only of a list of subjects, not only of statements of the content of these subjects expressed in terms of 'knowledge, skills and understanding' and 'matters, skills and processes', but also of detailed statements of levels of attainment regarded as the norm for pupils at four key stages in their period of compulsory education – 7+, 11+, 14+ and 16+ – and of an elaborate structure of assessment arrangements to discover whether pupils have reached the appropriate levels at each key stage.

THE IMPLEMENTATION OF THE NATIONAL CURRICULUM

Curriculum and assessment councils

Next we should note that section 7(1) of the Act creates three councils whose task it is to attend to the implementation and the monitoring of various aspects of these new policies:

(a) a body corporate known as the National Curriculum Council;

(b) a body corporate known as the Curriculum Council for Wales; and

(c) a body corporate known as the School Examinations and Assessment Council.

Each of these councils is to have a membership of not less than ten or more than fifteen, who are to be appointed by the Secretary of State. This membership 'shall include persons having relevant knowledge and experience in education' (1988 Act, s. 7(2)), although there is no indication of how many such persons should be included.

The general functions of the National Curriculum Council (NCC), and of the Curriculum Council for Wales in relation to Wales, are set out in section 7(3) of the Act:

(a) to keep all aspects of the curriculum for maintained schools under review;
(b) to advise the Secretary of State on such matters concerned with the curriculum for maintained schools as he may refer to it or as it may see fit;
(c) to advise the Secretary of State on, and if so requested by him assist him to carry out, programmes of research and development for purposes connected with the curriculum for schools; and
(d) to publish and disseminate, and to assist in the publication and dissemination of, information relating to the curriculum for schools.

The functions of the School Examinations and Assessment Council (SEAC) are contained in section 7(4):

(a) to keep all aspects of examinations and assessment under review;
(b) to advise the Secretary of State on such matters concerned with examinations and assessment as he may refer to it or as it may see fit;
(c) to advise the Secretary of State on, and if so requested by him assist him to carry out, programmes of research and development for purposes connected with examinations and assessment;
(d) to publish and disseminate, and to assist in the publication and dissemination of, information relating to examinations and assessment;
(e) to make arrangements with appropriate bodies for the moderation of assessments made in pursuance of assessment arrangements; and
(f) to advise the Secretary of State on the exercise of his powers under section 5(1) of this Act [that negative clause we noted earlier which requires schools to obtain approval for 'a qualification authenticated by an outside person'].

It is perhaps worth noting further that 'there is no requirement upon SEAC to consult, though in contrast the National Curriculum Council does have to consult about the nature of the curriculum proposals' (Nuttall, 1989, p. 44).

These, then, are the duties of the bodies which have been established to attend to the implementation of the National Curriculum and of its associated assessment programme. We must now look at how they have tackled this task and at what has been done since the Act became law to ensure its effective implementation.

Task Group on Assessment and Testing

It will be apparent that the regular assessment of pupils is a crucial element in this form of national curriculum; it will also be apparent that, for this elaborate programme of regular assessment to be carried out, two main tasks have first to be tackled: the establishment of appropriate attainment targets in relation to agreed programmes of study in each subject area; and the creation of an approved framework for the assessment of pupils in relation to those attainment targets. Both these tasks have been addressed during the period since the passing of the Act, and indeed immediately beforehand, and we must now look closely at what has been done in relation to them. Proposals which have been made and action taken in relation to the assessment framework must be considered first, however, since these were being framed before the Act became law and they have created the base upon which other elements of the structure have been built.

That base consists for the most part of the proposals made in the reports of the Task Group on Assessment and Testing (TGAT) (DES, 1988a, 1988b), a group set up in July 1987 to 'advise on the practical considerations governing assessment within the National Curriculum' (DES 1987, para. 1). The group submitted its main report in December 1987 and three supplementary reports in June 1988.

The main report begins by claiming (although, as we shall see later, it is by no means as self-evidently true as seems to be implied) that:

A school can function effectively only if it has adopted:
- clear aims and objectives;
- ways of gauging the achievement of these;
- comprehensible language for communicating the extent of those achievements to pupils, their parents and teachers, and to the wider community, so that everyone involved can take informed decisions about future action.

(DES, 1988a, para. 2)

It then proceeds to set out four general criteria of assessment to which it recommends that 'for the purpose of national assessment we give priority' (op. cit., para. 5). These four criteria it describes as follows:

- the assessment results should give direct information about pupils' achievement in relation to objectives: they should be *criterion-referenced*;
- the results should provide a basis for decisions about pupils' further learning needs: they should be *formative*;
- the scales or grades should be capable of comparison across classes and schools, if teachers, pupils and parents are to share a common language and common standards: so the assessments should be calibrated or *moderated*;
- the ways in which criteria and scales are set up and used should relate to expected routes of educational development, giving some continuity to a pupil's assessment at different ages: the assessments should relate to *progression*.

(DES, 1988a, para. 5)

It is also stressed later that the group's brief has been to ensure that the information derived from assessments (including tests):

shall be capable of serving several purposes:
- *formative*, so that the positive achievements of a pupil may be recognised and discussed and the appropriate next steps may be planned;
- *diagnostic*, through which learning difficulties may be scrutinised and classified so that appropriate remedial help and guidance can be provided;
- *summative*, for the recording of the overall achievement of a pupil in a systematic way;
- *evaluative*, by means of which some aspects of the work of a school, an LEA or other discrete part of the educational service can be assessed and/or reported upon.

(op. cit., para. 23)

On the basis of that rationale, the report goes on to explore many aspects of assessment, especially its potential impact on teaching and learning; to claim that no system yet constructed meets all four of the criteria listed; and to offer a set of recommendations which it believes will ensure that the system to be introduced in parallel with the National Curriculum will do so, and will at the same time meet all the demands that are to be placed on the information which will be gleaned in this way.

The report concludes by listing its recommendations under three main headings: 'Purposes and Principles', 'The Assessment System in Practice' and 'Implementation'. To attempt to summarize these recommendations is to risk failing to do them justice. However, the following would seem to be the most important points made in them.

In relation to the purposes and principles of the system, it is first recommended that the system should be 'essentially formative' (op. cit., para. 227), but also alive to the need for 'more detailed diagnostic assessment' (ibid.). At 16+, however, it should also be summative. 'For summative and evaluative purposes results should be aggregated across classes and schools so that no individual performances can be separated out' (op. cit., recommendation 3). All information about individuals is to be treated as confidential and made available only to those who need to have it in order to help and support those individuals. 'Teachers' ratings of pupil performance should be used as a fundamental element of the national assessment system' (op. cit., recommendation 11), and these 'should be moderated in such a way as to convey and to inform national standards' (op. cit., recommendation 13), so that the system will 'be based on a combination of moderated teachers' ratings and standardised assessment tasks' (op. cit., recommendation 14). This means that there must be developed a national system of 'standard assessment tasks', covering a wide range of 'modes of presentation, operation and response' (op. cit., recommendation 7), and 'so designed that flexibility of form and use is allowed wherever this can be consistent with national comparability of results' (ibid.). Furthermore, a mixture of such test instruments should be used 'in order to minimise curriculum distortion' (op. cit., recommendation 10).

In practice, such national assessment is to be undertaken at 7+, 11+, 14+ and 16+, and the reporting to occur near the end of the school year. The results of these assessments for any individual pupil 'should be confidential, to be discussed between pupil, parents and teachers, and to be otherwise transmitted in confidence' (op. cit., recommendation 29). 'National assessment results for a class as a whole and a school as a whole should be available to the parents of its pupils' (ibid.). 'The only form in which results . . . for, and identifying, a given school should be published should be as part of a broader report by that school of its work as a whole' (op. cit., recommendation 30). And any such report 'should include a general report for the area, prepared by the local authority, to indicate the nature of socio-economic and other influences which are known to affect schools' (op. cit., recommendation 31). National assessment results, aggregated at school level, should be reported in this form at every key stage except the first (7+). It is worth noting, however, that, while accepting this, the Secretary of State has subsequently strongly recommended that schools should nevertheless publish the results of seven-year-olds.

Two additional points should be noted. First, there is the recommendation that GCSE (i.e. the present system of assessment at 16+) 'should be retained in its present form until the national assessment system is initiated at earlier ages' (op. cit., recommendation 24), but that 'eventually changes will be necessary to the GCSE and other criteria' (op. cit., recommendation 37). The Secretary of State has subsequently announced that GCSE will be the future form of assessment at 16+, especially in the core subjects, and, more recently, that the GCSE grading system will be merged with the ten-level scale, which we shall see later has been devised for the new attainment targets, level 4 being the minimal pass level and level 10 being of a higher standard than the current GCSE Grade A. It has also been announced that as part of this reorganization all subjects must have written examinations as an element in the assessment of pupils at this stage.

Second, we should note that particular mention is made in the TGAT report of the potential impact of this new system on children with special educational needs, the report's recommendations being that 'wherever children with special educational needs are capable of undertaking the national tests, they should be encouraged to do so' (op. cit., recommendation 38), and that 'a special unit within a chosen test development agency should be dedicated to producing test materials and devising testing and assessment procedures sufficiently wide-ranging and sensitive to respond to the needs of these children' (op. cit., recommendation 39).

With regard to implementation, the prime need clearly has to be the specification of what is to be assessed in each subject. An earlier recommendation of the report had suggested that each subject 'should report a small number (preferably no more than four and never more than six) of profile components' (op. cit., recommendation 6). These profile components should reflect 'the variety of knowledge, skills and understanding to which the subject gives rise' (ibid.), and they must also be weighted in ways which reflect what is perceived as their relative importance. It is also necessary to 'define a sequence of levels in each of its profile components, related to broad criteria for progression in that component (op. cit., recommendation 20). Where a profile component is regarded as applying over the full range from 7+ to 16+, the report recommends that there should be ten such levels. This kind of specification is essential of course if the assessment system is to be criterion-referenced.

The second major need is for the development of appropriate tests, 'standard assessment tasks', for each profile component at each key stage. Teachers must also be given help and advice to enable them to make their own internal assessments against comparable criteria; they must be provided with appropriate in-service support. Finally, it is recommended that the system 'should be phased in over a period adequate for the preparation and trial of new assessment methods, for teacher preparation, and for pupils to benefit from extensive experience of the new curriculum' (op. cit., recommendation 44). The period suggested is 'at least five years from the promulgation of the relevant attainment targets' (ibid.).

The group subsequently published its second document, *Three Supplementary Reports* (DES, 1988b). These represent a response to comments made on the first report and further explication of some of the proposals made there, but the view expressed is that 'none of the criticisms voiced has been sufficient to cause the Group to revise its recommendations significantly' (op. cit., p. 1).

It will be clear from this brief summary of the work of the TGAT group that every effort has been made to minimize the possible negative effects of this kind of extensive programme of assessment on the educational experience of pupils. It may also be apparent, however, that this has been done only at the expense of adopting, uncritically, a particular view of education, of the curriculum and of subjects within that curriculum, a view which, as we shall see later, is far from being unproblematic. At the practical level, it will also be clear what the next steps in its implementation must be, and it is to these that we now turn.

As we have just seen, two parallel developments become necessary if the kind of scheme we have seen outlined is to be implemented effectively. First, all subjects within the National Curriculum need to be defined in terms of profile components, levels of attainment, attainment targets (ATs) and programmes of study. Second, standard assessment tasks (SATs) need to be developed to test pupils' attainments in relation to these targets at each key stage. The first of these tasks has been undertaken by a number of subject working groups, each looking at a particular subject area.

The subject working groups and statutory orders

Working groups of this kind were established by the National Curriculum Council for the 'core' subjects, mathematics, science and English, and have now completed their work and reported their conclusions. These have been considered by the Council and by the Secretary of State. Agreed proposals have been published for consultation purposes and these are being translated into statutory orders, that is, they are being given the force of law. These orders prescribe attainment targets and programmes of study for each of these subjects at each key stage. They are intended to determine the minimum requirements in each subject and to allow for the fact that what is taught in practice may go much wider. They also deliberately refrain from prescribing teaching methods or approaches, textbooks or other teaching materials (DES, 1989d). Nor do they specify the amount of time to be devoted to each subject, other than by requiring that 'a reasonable time' be allocated to each. It is also claimed that they will offer scope for the teaching of other subjects and for cross-curricular issues.

Similar working groups are gradually being established to do the same job for the other foundation subjects, although here the statutory requirements will be less detailed than for the core subjects, and those for music, art and physical education are expected to be very broad. And so, when this task is completed, what is seen as the essential content of every subject in the National Curriculum will have been defined in terms of a progression of attainment targets, programmes of study and levels of attainment within several profile components.

It would be too cumbersome, and perhaps unnecessary, to attempt here to outline in detail the proposals of each of these working groups or even of the orders which they have led to. A very brief summary of one or two, however, may be helpful in indicating the kind of flesh which has been put on to those skeletal proposals we have so far considered.

For example, the proposals resulting from the work of the working group on English (DES, 1989a) have identified three profile components: reading; writing; and speaking and listening. These have then been translated into five attainment targets:

Profile Component 1 – Speaking and listening
    Attainment target 1
        The development of pupils' understanding of the spoken word and the capacity to express themselves effectively, in a variety of speaking and listening activities, matching style and response to audience and purpose.
Profile Component 2 – Reading
    Attainment target 2
        The development of the ability to read, understand and respond to all types of writing, as well as the development of information-retrieval strategies for the purposes of study.

Profile Component 3 – Writing
  Attainment target 3
    A growing ability to construct and convey meaning in written language matching style to audience and purpose.
  Attainment target 4
    Spelling (up to level 4)
  Attainment target 5
    Handwriting (up to level 4)
  Attainment target 4/5
    Presentation (level 5 and above)

(DES, 1989a, Appendix)

Furthermore,

for each attainment target there are statements of attainment which define up to ten levels of attainment specifying what pupils should know, understand and be able to do, appropriate for pupils of different ages and abilities. The Report also recommends the ranges of levels of attainment which should apply to pupils at the end of each of key stages 2, 3 and 4 – i.e. at the ages of 11, 14 and 16. These are:
  Key stage 2 – Levels 2 to 5
  Key stage 3 – Levels 3 to 8
  Key stage 4 – Levels 3 to 10

(op. cit., para. 6)

These details are in turn backed by proposals for programmes of study for each key stage.

This structure has, after discussion and some subsequent refinement, been translated into an order in respect of attainment targets and programmes of study for key stage 1 (7+) which came into effect in August 1989. Similar orders will in due course be established for the other key stages.

Similarly, the report on design and technology (DES, 1989b) has identified two profile components – one for design and technology and one for information technology – with four attainment targets in the first profile component and one in the second. These are:

Profile Component 1 – Design and Technology
  AT1 – Identifying needs and opportunities
    Through exploration and investigation of a range of contexts (home; school; recreation; community; business and industry) pupils should be able to identify and state clearly needs and opportunities for design and technological activities.
  AT2 – Generating a design proposal
    Pupils should be able to produce a realistic, appropriate and achievable design by generating, exploring and developing design and technological ideas and by refining and detailing the design proposal they have chosen.
  AT3 – Planning and making
    Working to a plan derived from their previously developed design, pupils should be able to identify, manage and use appropriate resources, including both knowledge and processes in order to make an artefact, system or environment.

AT4 – Appraising
  Pupils should be able to develop, communicate and act constructively upon an appraisal of the processes, outcomes and effects of their own design and technological activity as well as of the outcomes and effects of the design and technological activity of others, including those from other times and cultures.
Profile Component 2 – Information Technology
  AT – IT
  Pupils should be able to use IT appropriately and effectively to communicate and handle information in a variety of forms and for a variety of purposes and to design, develop and evaluate appropriate models of real or imaginary situations.

(DES, 1989b, p. v)

The group has then defined ten levels of attainment for each attainment target and has recommended that these levels should relate to key stages on the following scheme:

Key Stage 1 – Levels 1–3
Key Stage 2 – Levels 2–5
Key Stage 3 – Levels 3–7
Key Stage 4 – Levels 4–10

(op. cit., p. iii)

This report was published only in June 1989, so that orders have not yet been established, but they will be in due course in the same way as is happening in other areas.

These detailed statements of profile components, programmes of study, attainment targets and levels for each subject area thus provide the basis for the development of test instruments, of standard assessment tasks (SATs), a process which is now also under way.

The development of Standard Assessment Tasks

While the National Curriculum Council has been supervising the work just described, the other major council, the School Examinations and Assessment Council (SEAC), has, among other things, been making arrangements for the development of test instruments to enable assessment to take place at the designated key stages.

It has been decided that the first full national exercise in such assessment will be conducted at key stage 1 (7+), so that this is where the attention was originally directed. In December 1988 contracts were issued, on the advice of SEAC, to three of the agencies which had submitted proposals for undertaking this work. The brief of these agencies was to develop three sample SATs each by December 1989, so that these can be trialled, piloted in the summer of 1990 and used for a 'first unreported run' (FUR) in the school year 1990/91. If this is successful, they will then be used for the first full and proper assessment exercise in 1991/92, and the results of this will be reported. As we noted earlier, the publication of aggregated results will not be required of schools at this stage, but the Secretary of State has strongly recommended it.

The agencies developing these SATs are expected to negotiate with schools so that a sample group of six-year-old pupils will use the National Curriculum attainment targets and programmes of study in 1989 in preparation for this piloting exercise. It is further required of them that the SATs they develop should be cross-curricular, since it is hoped that the subject base of the National Curriculum and its assessment programme will not impose too tight a subject focus on the curriculum of the first or infant schools, although those SATs must give clear indications of the levels of attainment reached in the core subjects.

Subsequently, contracts have also been issued to several agencies for the development of SATs for key stage 3 (14+), which is the next stage at which it is planned to introduce the assessment arrangements. Here the focus is on the four major subjects of the National Curriculum – mathematics, science, English and design and technology – and separate contracts have been issued in relation to each of these subjects. It is hoped, however, that the agencies involved in this work will collaborate with one another to produce cross-curricular assessment instruments. These agencies are expected to produce sample SATs for piloting in January 1991.

In preparation for the full implementation of this assessment programme at key stages 1 and 3, the programmes of study and attainment targets in the three core subjects were introduced for all pupils entering key stage 1, i.e. entering infant or first schools, in autumn 1989, and at the same date those in mathematics and science for pupils entering key stage 3.

All these agencies will also have the task of developing materials and programmes for the in-service training of teachers, so that the teachers will be able to fulfil effectively and efficiently their role in the assessment process. The in-service training of teachers is one of the most important of the other developments currently going ahead in preparation for the full implementation of these new policies. It is to a consideration of several of these that we must now turn.

Other developments

It should be noted that the new system became fully operative for all pupils in key stages 1 to 3 (i.e. those aged five to fourteen) in autumn 1989, so that a number of significant agencies need to be prepared for the massive changes, and in some cases the additional work, which now face them. Teachers, as we have just indicated, need a good deal of in-service support. This is currently being offered, in part at least, in the form of information pamphlets emerging from the DES and from the NCC and SEAC. The DES, for example, issued its leaflet,

National Curriculum: From Policy to Practice, in 1989 (DES, 1989c) and said of it, in its Introduction, 'The booklet is designed as a guide for heads and other teachers. It will amplify what is said in DES Circulars sent to head teachers in connection with their new statutory responsibilities; and serve also as a work of reference for all teachers about the effects of the new requirements and the issues which will arise as they are put into practice.'

It seems unlikely that teachers can be adequately prepared for their new roles by this kind of publication alone. And in view of the current official policies in relation to the initial training of teachers, with their emphasis on practice rather than theory, it is surprising that the DES or Her Majesty's Inspectorate (HMI) is prepared to claim any efficacy for this kind of publication in developing practical classroom skills. However, the document itself sets out some of the back-up arrangements that have been made. It tells us, for example, that 'NCC is now supporting a programme of general familiarisation and more specific training for the introduction of the first attainment targets and programmes of study – to be followed by training to help teachers with the new assessment arrangements' (DES, 1989c, para. 9.10). Many local authorities, it goes on to tell us, are using funds available under the training grant scheme for this purpose and for in-service training ('Baker') days. (In this connection, it is interesting to note that many teachers now call these 'B-days', since their perception of what happens on such occasions is that a great mass of material strikes them with a great 'whoosh'!) Two additional such days were made available to all schools for this purpose during 1989. HMI has also been running courses and conferences, but again the potential efficacy of these must be questioned in the light of its own views of the methods appropriate for the initial training of teachers, which, as we saw just now, stress practice and ignore, or even dispute, the value of theory.

One must also have reservations about how much can be achieved in the occasional Baker day, especially when so often these seem to be examples of the blind, or at best the partly sighted, leading the blind. It is possible, and indeed it is to be hoped, that the INSET arrangements which are to be an essential part of the programmes of SAT development may be more substantial and may lead to more effective forms of teacher preparation. Much, however, needs to be done in this area – and none of it is assisted by the current shortage of qualified teaching staff, and even less, it should perhaps be added, by the proposals to resolve this difficulty by the introduction of unqualified or partly qualified teachers.

Teachers, however, are not the only people who need to be assisted to meet the demands of the new policies. The 1988 Act lays additional duties on local authorities and on governing bodies, since it specifically indicates their respon-sibility for the curriculum in the schools under their care and, especially, for ensuring that that curriculum meets the requirements of the Act. Again, therefore, documents are being issued and courses of instruction organized for those who now find themselves responsible for these new requirements and who need help to fulfil them adequately.

Parents, too, need to be informed of what is happening. Few parents are other than highly conservative when it comes to the education of their children. And many are seriously concerned about what these new policies will mean, not merely for society but for their own individual offspring. Thus efforts are being made to provide information for them too; for all parents, that is, and not merely for those who happen to have the additional role and duties of parent–governors.

Much work is being done, then, but much more work of a more appropriate and effective kind needs to be done, to prepare a range of people for the changes which have been necessitated by the new policies.

OTHER ASSOCIATED ASPECTS OF THE NEW POLICIES

It must not be forgotten that there are many other changes taking place in the school system as a result of the 1988 Act, changes which, although they must have their own impact on the curriculum of every school, go beyond that and affect its structure and management. It would be wrong to ignore these in outlining the main features of the National Curriculum, since not only do they create additional burdens for those responsible for implementing that curriculum, they also provide the context for its implementation and impinge upon it in several other ways.

Perhaps the most important, and the most significant, of the other provisions of the 1988 Act are that concerning the possibility of schools 'opting out' of the jurisdiction of their local authorities, in some cases by having themselves established as city technology colleges (CTCs); that for the local financial management of schools, placing responsibility for the distribution of funds and other resources on the headteacher and the governing body of each school; and that concerning the requirement that schools and their governing bodies provide detailed reports of the curriculum for which they are responsible.

Information to be provided by headteachers and governing bodies

As a part of the in-service arrangements we considered earlier, the DES has advised that all schools prepare their own National Curriculum development plans, 'which will look over the early years of implementation of the National Curriculum and show how schools' staffing and other resources will need to adapt to meet the new challenges' (DES, 1989c, para. 9.12). The stated purpose of such plans is 'to ensure that it [the curriculum] meets overall objectives as well as specific statutory requirements, and that concentration on the latter does not crowd out adequate attention to other subjects and issues' (ibid.).

There are, however, several other requirements which have statutory force. The governing body of every school must provide detailed particulars of the school's curriculum, including such things as a summary of the content of the school's curriculum, how foundation subjects are organized and what other subjects and cross-curricular themes are included. The governors must also produce an annual report to parents and submit a copy of this to the local education authority responsible for the school, or, in the case of schools which have 'opted out' and are grant-maintained, to the Secretary of State. It must, by 30 June in every year, make available to the local authority statistical details of the educational provision made during the current school year, and, by the same date, the headteacher must inform the governing body of plans for the educational provision to be made in the next following school year. These statistical details are to include such things as the subjects or courses taught, the number of hours per week for each of these, the length of time of each course in weeks, the number of pupils following each course and the grouping criteria used. Detailed forms of guidance have been made available for these purposes.

Local management of schools

The 1988 Act also requires the delegation to individual school governing bodies of responsibility for the management of the school's budget in all cases except that of schools whose total roll of pupils falls below 200 registrations. The local authority must submit to the Secretary of State for his or her approval a scheme for the distribution of funding to its schools according to a clear formula. Such a scheme must accord with the Secretary of State's guidance and requirements. Once this scheme has been approved, the authority must make the agreed sums available to each governing body.

By section 25(5) of the 1988 Act, the governing body then:

(a) shall be entitled, subject to any provision made by or under the scheme, to spend any sum made available to them in respect of the budget share for any financial year as they think fit for the purposes of the school; and

(b) may delegate to the head teacher, to such extent as may be permitted by or under the scheme, their power under paragraph (a) above in relation to any part of that sum.

Once a governing body has received its financial allocation in this way, it becomes responsible for meeting all the school's costs (except those incurred by the provision and supervision of school meals) from within this budget. This expressly includes the provision of teaching and non-teaching staff, which under former policies was the responsibility of the local authority. However, it is required, in deciding on the allocation of this budget to various heads, to 'comply in spending that sum with such reasonable conditions as the authority thinks fit to impose' (1988 Act, s. 35(4)), and its annual report must include a financial statement indicating how its budget for the year has been used.

Under the previous system, the major costs for each school, and in particular those arising from the payment of teaching and non-teaching staff, were met by the local authority; and the school's budget, i.e. that proportion of its funding over which the headteacher and the governors were able to exercise jurisdiction, was relatively small, covering mainly non-staffing resources. Under the new system, however, in most schools the headteacher and governing body will be responsible, albeit under the general supervision of the local authority – and ultimately of the Secretary of State – for the complete financial management of the institution. This change has many possible implications, not least in so far as it offers governing bodies a discretion they did not previously enjoy in relation to the numbers of teachers and other staff they will employ. However, its prime relevance here relates to the additional adjustments it requires from governing bodies, headteachers and schools who are already endeavouring to cope with the demands of implementing the National Curriculum, and, further, the implications it has for the manner in which that implementation may be undertaken and carried out.

Grant-maintained status

We must further note the parallel facility which the 1988 Act offers for governing bodies to 'opt out' of the control or supervision of local authorities, even that reduced control and supervision we have just noted, and apply for grant-maintained status, i.e. to be funded directly by the Secretary of State.

Any school which by virtue of its size qualifies for the kind of self-managing rights we have just been discussing may, if it wishes, apply for grant-maintained status and independence of its local authority. To achieve this status, the governing body must hold a secret, postal ballot of parents – either on its own decision or in response to a written request. Full details of the intention to hold such a ballot must be provided for all interested parties, especially parents. Should that ballot result in a majority in favour of seeking grant-maintained status, detailed proposals for this must be published and a copy sent to the Secretary of State. These proposals must cover all aspects of the application as these are set out in the Act. During a period of two months from the publication of these proposals, various named parties may submit objections to them to the Secretary of State. These interested parties are listed in section 46(8) of the Act as:

(a) any ten or more local government electors for the area of the local education authority by whom the school is maintained;
(b) the trustees (if any) of the school concerned;
(c) the governing body of any school affected by the proposals; and
(d) any local education authority concerned.

During the same period the Secretary of State must reach a decision. Under section 46(9) he or she:

(a) may reject any proposals under this section; or
(b) where a school in respect of which such proposals are made is eligible for grant-maintained status on the date of publication of the proposals, may approve them without modification or, after consultation with the existing governing body, approve them with such modifications as he thinks desirable.

Thus maintained schools may break away completely from local authority control or guidance and become answerable directly to the Secretary of State. This involves direct funding and acceptance of the detailed requirements relating to the government and management of the school. Again, therefore, we have a further element in the Act which must have major implications for the ambience of and the context for the implementation of the National Curriculum.

City technology colleges

In this connection it is finally worth noting that the further possibility exists for some secondary schools to acquire funding from outside commercial sources and to become established as independent schools and known as city technology colleges (CTCs). Certain characteristics of such schools are prescribed in section 80(2) of the 1988 Act. These are that each such school:

(a) is situated in an urban area;
(b) provides education free of charge for pupils of different abilities who have attained the age of eleven years but not the age of nineteen years and who are wholly or mainly drawn from the area in which the school is situated; and
(c) has a broad curriculum with an emphasis on science and technology.

Some state funding will be provided for such a school, but an outside body must contract to 'establish and maintain, and to carry on or provide for the carrying on' (1988 Act, s. 80(1)) of every school granted this status.

It is worth noting that this strategy has failed to attract commercial or industrial funding on the scale originally envisaged, so that a much larger input of public money will be needed to support those schools which have applied for this status.

What is perhaps of most importance here, however, is that such schools, in becoming thus largely independent of public funding, join those independent schools which already exist in being excluded from the requirements of the National Curriculum, although all independent schools have been recommended to adopt it.

More implications for Control — Finance + power.

Disapplication

One further provision of the 1988 Act must be noted before we conclude our summary of its main features and requirements. It will be clear from what has already been said that the focus of its provisions is on some concept its authors have of the 'normal' child, and that it may not, as a result, offer an appropriate context, scheme or curriculum for the education of those pupils deemed to have special educational needs, those who under the terms of the 1981 Education Act would be 'statemented' – officially declared to be in need of special provision of one kind or another. We should perhaps also note that, since the estimate made in the Warnock Report (DES, 1978a) was that around 20 per cent of pupils might fall into this category at some stage in their educational career, this is by no means a minor problem, even if one is looking at the schooling system from the outside and from a distance (it is, of course, a major problem for those on the inside and especially those who are responsible for pupils who might be regarded as being in this position). One short paragraph in the 1988 Act (s. 10) may therefore seem to be somewhat less than adequate for the institution of a scheme for dealing with an issue of this scale.

The solution proffered in that paragraph is that of modification or 'disapplication', although the Act itself does not provide any kind of detailed explanation of what this entails. The consultative document (DES, 1987, p. 15) forewarned that 'for a pupil who has a statement of special need under the Education Act 1981, it is proposed that the statement should specify any national curriculum requirements which should not apply'. And section 10 of the Act itself says: 'A statement under section 7 of the 1981 Act of a pupil's special educational needs may direct that the provisions of the National Curriculum shall apply as respects the pupil with such modifications as may be specified in the statement.'

The follow-up information and advice offered by the DES document, *National Curriculum: From Policy To Practice* (DES, 1989c), fleshes out these rather stark statements in several ways. First, it points out that 'all pupils share the same statutory entitlement to a broad and balanced curriculum, including access to the National Curriculum' (op. cit., para. 8.1). Second, it suggests that 'virtually *all* pupils will be able to record some progress through these levels' (op. cit., para. 8.2) (i.e. the ten levels of attainment determined for each subject area, as we noted earlier). This is particularly true, it goes on to suggest, since 'teachers are free to determine their own teaching approaches and ways of delivering the programmes' (ibid.), so that this 'will allow for different ways of doing things to help, for example, those with a physical or sensory handicap' (ibid.). It further points out that they might be taught in a mixed-age class – a clear indication that such children are viewed as being merely 'slower' than other children and thus requiring provision which reflects nothing more than a difference of pace (and, further, a hint that we might soon see the reinvention of the elementary school system of grouping by 'standards'). Third, however, it recognizes that 'the flexibility outlined above will not cover all cases' (op. cit., para. 8.3). Adaptation thus becomes necessary, and three forms of such adaptation are outlined:

> *For groups of pupils defined in terms of particular cases and circumstances*: by including exemptions or modifications in the Orders which lay down the attainment targets, programmes of study, assessment arrangements and in the information requirements – or by making special regulations to exempt such a group of pupils or modify their curricula.
>
> *For individual pupils with continuing special educational needs which are covered by a statement under the 1981 Act*: by using the statement to modify or disapply National Curriculum requirements.
>
> *For individual pupils for whom the National Curriculum is temporarily inappropriate, including those awaiting the preparation of a statement or a reassessment under the 1981 Act*: by enabling the headteacher to disapply or modify the National Curriculum in circumstances set out in regulations.
>
> (DES, 1989c, para. 8.4)

Further elaboration of these forms of adaptation is given, and from this we learn that they will include the possibility of excluding the results of the testing and assessments of such pupils in published statements of a school's results, and also of the disapplication or modification of the assessment requirements even when the attainment targets and programmes of study continue to apply – a strange arrangement, since the concept of an unassessed attainment target is especially odd.

Finally, we are told that 'how this will work in detail will be set out in regulations, after consultations' (op. cit., para. 8.11). In general, however, it is suggested that headteachers will need to notify and explain to their governing bodies, the parents of the child concerned and the local authority (when they have one) the reasons for and the details of any action taken under these provisions.

SUMMARY AND CONCLUSIONS

This chapter has attempted to set out, largely without comment, the details of the National Curriculum, the policies related to it and the steps so far taken to implement it in our schools. To maintain its intention to describe, rather than, at this stage, to offer any kind of judgement or evaluation, a good deal of reliance has been placed on quotations from the official documents which have set out, publicized and elaborated these new policies.

It is hoped that it has in this way provided a statement of those policies which is sufficiently full, factual and objective to constitute a basis for the evaluation of these policies which subsequent chapters will undertake.

2

THE NATIONAL CURRICULUM IN ITS
HISTORICAL SETTING

If one wished to be unkind, one would begin a chapter on the historical antece-
dents of the National Curriculum by drawing attention to the fact that 'the most
striking feature of the . . . national curriculum is that it is at least 83 years old'
(Aldrich, 1988, p. 22) in so far as it is in every major respect identical with that in
the regulations, issued in 1904 by the Board of Education, which prescribed the
curriculum for state secondary schools. 'There is such a striking similarity
between these . . . that it appears that one was simply copied from the other'
(ibid.). One major difference is that this curriculum, originally devised for grammar schools, 'is now to be extended to primary and comprehensive secondary
schools' (op. cit., p. 239).

Further, as Richard Aldrich goes on to point out, the fact that the National
Curriculum is essentially concerned with testing, as we saw in Chapter 1, suggests that 'the historical antecedent is clearly the Revised Code of 1862' (ibid.),
'a system of payment by results' (ibid.), introduced by Robert Lowe, a 'member
of a government which was determined to reduce central expenditure on elementary education' (ibid.), a system 'whereby grants to schools were based upon
standards of attainment reached by children in a very limited range of subjects'
(ibid.). At various points in later chapters we shall see the impact of that on the
quality of educational provision, at least as it appeared to Matthew Arnold.

We cannot explore here these issues in great historical detail. However, the
National Curriculum and the arrangements for its implementation, which were
described in the previous chapter, must be viewed in the general context of the
historical development both of attempts to theorize about educational provision

and of the efforts which have been made in the United Kingdom, since the advent of state-provided educational facilities, to translate such theorizing into practice. Chapter 3 will attempt to analyse and to identify the conceptual underpinning of the National Curriculum, its goals, its philosophy, its values. In preparation for that discussion, this chapter will endeavour to pick out some of the different, sometimes conflicting, views of education which have been expressed, or even merely assumed, and to draw attention to the clash of these views reflected in the attempts to implement a state system of education in the United Kingdom. For we can sensibly attempt an evaluation of the rationale of the new policies only against the backcloth of what they have replaced and in the context of the differing philosophies that have been competing for dominance.

To do this it will be helpful if we first explore the variety of views which have been, and continue to be, expressed about the role and purpose of education in society, the range of meanings which can be seen to be, and to have been, given to the term 'education'.

CONCEPTS OF EDUCATION

There are several strata of philosophical complexity at which one can explore the issue of differing concepts of education. It may be useful to begin, however, by noting one major distinction: that between instrumental and intrinsic views of the educational process. From the very outset, discussions of education, beginning with that in Plato's *Republic*, have recognized an important distinction between what education may be seen to be *for* and what it *is*, between the idea of using education to turn children into certain kinds of adult and that of using it to support their personal development as individuals, between using the education system to serve the needs of society, whether these are seen in social/political or in technological/commercial terms, and using it to promote the growth of the individual. Indeed, it has been argued (Peters, 1965, 1966) that terms like 'training', 'instruction', even 'indoctrination', have been coined to describe these instrumental uses of schools and schooling, while the term 'education' is to be distinguished from these expressly by its being confined to those teaching activities meant to support personal development or initiation into activities which are pursued for their own sake, activities regarded as being of value in themselves rather than through what they might lead to. Thus a distinction is drawn between teaching pupils those subjects which are socially or commercially useful and introducing them to activities, experiences, aspects of their cultural heritage which it is felt may enhance their lives, extend their horizons and contribute to the development of their full potential as human beings.

The complexities of this debate, however, will already have begun to emerge. For it will be clear that this is not a distinction which it is easy to draw in all circumstances. It will be obvious, too, that both in theory and in practice these two, apparently quite distinct, goals or purposes will be difficult to distinguish completely. It will also be plain that much hinges on what we mean by 'individual or personal development', by 'cultural heritage', by 'enhancing lives', by 'extending horizons', by 'developing full potential as human beings'. It is also the case that, as in Plato's theory, many people have felt that, while training children for specific roles and tasks within society could not be justified within any concept of education, turning them into certain kinds of adult was and is precisely what education should be about, since for some people there is only one kind of acceptable human form and it is towards that that we should help children to strive.

Thus another kind of distinction begins to emerge, that between the development of the individual as an individual, enjoying freedom to make his or her own life decisions and to take charge of his or her own destiny, and the idea of development towards some ideal conception of adulthood, whether this be that of Plato's 'philosopher king', the medievalist's 'cultured gentleman', the Christian's 'God-fearing person' or of Marx's 'socialist or social "man"'.

Perhaps, therefore, we should now attempt to pick out for slightly more detailed exploration several of the many issues this brief discussion has already raised.

There would appear to be a number of views one may take of the goals or purposes or the nature of the educational process. The first of these is that the prime concern of education should be with the economic health and welfare of society and the contribution pupils can and/or will make to these if they are assisted, or even compelled, to develop appropriate skills, and perhaps even attitudes too, as a preparation for adult citizenship. This is the central concern of child-rearing practices, whether formal or informal, in primitive societies, along with initiation into the accepted norms of society. Childhood is seen as a period of preparation for adult roles, a time to learn how to fish, to hunt, to fight, to make weapons, to till the fields, to plant seed, to harvest, and so on. This continues to be the concern of most countries in the Third World, even when its focus has shifted to the needs of industry rather than of agriculture. It is also one concern, and sometimes the main concern, of the education system in societies one might regard as 'advanced', where it is often clear that vocational preparation continues to be the supreme consideration in educational planning and often, too, in the expectations which pupils and parents, as well as politicians and industrialists, have of educational provision.

Often, indeed some might argue always, this kind of obsession with the instrumental, the industrial/commercial and the vocational dimensions of the upbringing of children is also found to be closely associated with a second major view of education: that it should also be directed towards the socialization of children, towards initiating them into the norms and customs, the value system of society. Again, this is to be seen in its most obvious manifestations in the child-rearing practices of primitive societies, but, again too, it can be seen in the educational provision of the more advanced. In some societies, those which we would no doubt describe as totalitarian, there is little attempt to conceal that this is a major goal of the educational system, that it exists, at least in part, to instil in children certain values and attitudes, especially towards notions of the appropriate form of political order, to accept that their first loyalty is towards the state and their first duty to accept the political status quo. No doubt most of us would associate this in present times with the educational practices of the communist bloc, and would link it with comparable policies in relation to the control, through censorship, of the arts and the press. No doubt too, most of us would wish to call this indoctrination rather than education. If asked to give historical examples, we would perhaps most readily point to Nazi Germany and the Hitler Youth Movement and to comparable practices in Mussolini's Fascist Italy. In relation to these examples, it is interesting to note that the notion of a national curriculum was mooted and debated in the United Kingdom in the 1930s but was rejected then as smacking too much of totalitarianism – at that time a highly unpopular political doctrine for reasons which are not difficult to recognize.

It must be noted, however, that the use of the educational system for this kind of political end is not always as overt and blatant as in the examples just cited. In most societies deliberate attempts are made to use the educational system to promote certain kinds of social and political values – and religious values too, since it is plain that the massive contribution of the Churches to the development of educational provision over the years, along with their close involvement in the planning and management of schools and colleges, has been prompted at least as much by a desire to ensure that that provision should include the propagation of religious beliefs as by considerations of Christian charity. Indeed, it has been argued (Young, 1971) with some force and conviction that education must always and inevitably involve the inculcation of the values and beliefs – religious, moral, social and political – of those responsible for the planning of it, since those values and beliefs will be implicit in the content of that provision and in the criteria by which that content is selected. It is for this reason that some (Illich, 1971; Freire, 1972) have even argued for a 'deschooling' of society, since they have seen schools as the necessary agents of this process of political socialization and thus as major factors in the preservation of political systems deemed to be unsatisfactory.

Whether one accepts the force of this type of argument or not, however, there is no doubt that education systems can be used, and have been used, to promote particular value systems and even particular political beliefs, so that this must be recognized as a second major view of the purposes and goals of education, a second major concept of what education is and of what it is for.

Sometimes associated with this view is a third concept of education, one that deliberately eschews the kind of instrumentalism which is a major feature of both the views we have considered so far and defines education for us as some form of initiation into activities which are deemed to be intrinsically worthwhile, valuable in their own right and not in relation to what they lead to (Peters, 1965, 1966). The underlying assumption of this view is that there are certain things of eternal and undying value in the cultural heritage of society and that it is the prime purpose of education to make these available to pupils, to initiate them into the culture of society, to open their minds to what Matthew Arnold once called 'the best that has been thought and said', what might also be called 'high culture'. On this view, education is not about economic productivity, nor about vocational training, but about the transmission of what is aesthetically, morally and culturally best in society to subsequent generations. Its proponents would claim that its concern is with the quality of life in society rather than with the means by which that society is to sustain and maintain itself economically, with spiritual rather than economic values, with ends rather than means.

However, it was suggested at the beginning of the previous paragraph that this view is sometimes associated with the last view we considered, that education is, or should be, concerned to initiate children into the norms, values and beliefs of society. The reason for this is that it will be quickly apparent that nowhere are these norms, values and beliefs more effectively encapsulated than in a society's culture, and especially its 'high culture'. The important difference which would be claimed by those who advocate this view of education as initiation into one's cultural heritage, a difference which they would argue makes their theory one of education rather than indoctrination, is that the values implicit in this 'high culture', those they advocate we should deliberately set out to initiate pupils into, are timeless, eternal, objective and apolitical, in a way that more ephemeral political and social systems never can be. And so to initiate pupils into these is not in any sense to impose a value system on them but to introduce them to the very important concept of *human* values, those values which, they would claim, transcend particular societies and even particular historical contexts.

There is much that is attractive in such a view. Its concern is with what education *is* rather than with what it is *for*; it directs our attention towards the quality of life in society and away from the idea that it is acceptable to seek the means to an ever more affluent existence without giving any consideration to questions about how we might most valuably spend that existence, a form of society which Enoch Powell (1985) once described as 'a modern barbarism'. Its main drawback, however, is that its first and major premise is of doubtful validity; its assumption of timeless, objective status for the underpinning values of its concept of 'high culture' is highly questionable. And so, it falls foul of that problem we noted earlier, that, if values do not have this objective status, the imposition on children of any one form of education, of any one culture, will be a form of indoctrination into a particular set of values, again the values of those who control the education system and decide on its content.

This problem was not recognized as such when the value of 'high culture' remained largely unchallenged, and this view of education as providing access for all to the best of this 'high culture' became, and to a large extent continues to be, the basic principle of the Labour movement's educational policies. The problem has, however, in recent times begun to loom rather larger, especially in the context of a society which, it is freely accepted, is multicultural, pluralist in its cultures and thus in its value systems. For it is quite clear that there are major differences in the cultural heritage of many different groups in modern advanced societies, and that these major cultural differences reflect major differences of value systems too. One has only to think of the recent problems surrounding Salman Rushdie's novel, *The Satanic Verses*, to recognize the truth and indeed the significance of this. It thus becomes a highly questionable practice to impose the cultural heritage and the values of one of these groups, even of the majority group, on all children regardless of their cultural origins. Nor is this of doubtful validity only at the theoretical or philosophical level. At the practical level, too, it has become clear that many pupils will and do reject what they are offered in schools if it clearly is at odds with their own cultural background, and, indeed, especially if, as is often the case, it implies a rejection of, a disregard for, and even a 'rubbishing' of, that cultural heritage.

This is one reason why a fourth view of education and its purposes has emerged. It is a view which has been around, albeit perhaps only implicitly, even intuitively, for some time, but it has emerged with increased force in recent times. This is the view that education is the development of individual capacities and capabilities in a way that is not tied to the transmission of any particular view of culture or of values, indeed in a way that is specifically concerned to enable people to recognize, to challenge, to explore and to evaluate all views of culture and all value systems. On this view, education should set out to broaden horizons, to enrich life, to open up possibilities, to equip the individual to take advantage of these opportunities, to enhance awareness of the many dimensions of human existence, to raise levels of understanding, to encourage a critical and evaluative approach to all things and, above all, to promote a recognition of the importance of individual choice and to enable people to make such choices sensibly, thoughtfully and, especially, as autonomous individuals. Self-determination is the key concept of such a view.

This kind of view has also received a good deal of support in recent times from psychological studies of human development, which have revealed that we pass through several stages of development, but that, without the right kinds of educational stimulus, we can become stuck at any one of these stages, including the

first, and thus never reach the stage of fully autonomous thinking and the conceptual understanding upon which that must be based. To put this in the parlance of
more recent studies, we can, with the right kinds of educational experience,
develop a wide range of modes of understanding, or forms of representation, but,
without those experiences, we can remain for ever stunted in our intellectual
development and restricted both in our understanding and in our awareness of
many aspects of the world in which we live. Thus the role of education, on this
view, is clear: to provide the kinds of experience that will promote the fullest and
widest possible development of the individual's intellectual capacities and thus
of his or her control over his or her destiny.

Nor does an education conceived in this way need to be tied to or limited to
any one form of culture, or, indeed, to any one body of knowledge or collection
of school subjects. The focus of attention in educational planning, on this view,
shifts from the content of education to the subject of education, the child him- or
herself. Each child is to be provided with a set of educational experiences
selected to promote his or her development, to enhance his or her understanding,
to maximize his or her potential, to broaden his or her horizons, to extend his or
her capacity for autonomous and critical thinking, for self-determination. And it
is of no significance for anything other than the individual child's own requirements whether these experiences involve an exploration of Tudor England or of
Mogul India, of Christianity or of Islam, of Afro-Caribbean or of Anglo-Saxon
culture, of Chinese or of Greek mythology, of Western European or of Eastern
art. Indeed, the availability of all of these possibilities can of itself be a positive
advantage not only to the individual pupil but also to his or her fellow pupils,
since a widening of horizons is an essential element in this kind of intellectual
development.

Thus a very different view of education emerges, one whose focus is on what
the educational process can do for the individual child rather than on what it can
do for society, and one whose concern is with the continued development of the
human race rather than with its ossification at the point it has somehow already
succeeded in reaching. Its central concepts – development, understanding, potentialities, self-determination – are of course problematic, but one strength of this
view is that the problematic nature of its theoretical underpinning is recognized,
so that the view itself is seen as fluid and developing.

There are of course many more complexities to all these views than it has been
possible to bring out here. And there are dangers in offering them as 'ideal types'.
Three further general points must, therefore, be noted at this stage.

The first of these is that any of the four kinds of education we have identified
can be the result of our educational provision even if they are not explicitly its
intention. We can, as was suggested earlier, set out to offer pupils something
which is of value to them and succeed only in closing their minds and limiting

their prospects. Conversely, we can set out to offer a limited and limiting range of experiences, expressly designed to restrict the range of their thinking, only to discover that, human nature – thankfully – being what it is, some will escape our net and make up their own minds on all issues. That has been the encouraging message of much political science fiction, Orwell's *Nineteen Eighty–Four* and Huxley's *Brave New World* for example, as well as of all the actual attempts to govern the direction of the thinking of whole nations through the control of educational provision. We need to be aware, then, not only of what is intended in any scheme or policy for education but also of what its effects are likely to be.

The second general point to be noted is that, to some extent at least, systems can accommodate some, if not all, of the views of education we have listed, and may be able to reconcile some of their disparate goals. Some of them are clearly incompatible with one another; we cannot, for example, set out to socialize pupils into certain values, attitudes, beliefs and ways of thinking, while at the same time endeavouring to promote their development as autonomous, free-thinking, self-determined individuals. We can, on the other hand, quite reasonably set out to provide a form of education which offers vocational preparation and recognizes the need for an education system to cater for the economic requirements of society, while at the same time attempting to offer something of value to the individual recipient.

If this is our aim, the balance becomes crucial. Neither will it be possible to go very far without facing up to the need to declare priorities. We have already seen enough to know that these different views of education will lead to quite different forms of educational provision – different kinds of content, different school subjects, even to different views of the place of school subjects in education, and perhaps also to different kinds of structure to our educational system, whether we are to have selective grammar schools, for example, or city technology colleges, or comprehensive schools, or what. And some of the choices we make in the pursuit of one set of goals may well render the other goals inaccessible, as we have seen has already happened through failure to take proper account of cultural diversity. We might, therefore, set out to achieve a wide range of goals but, unless we are clear where our priorities lie, and, indeed, where our goals may be incompatible with one another, we are unlikely to achieve them, and may in fact, as some would say is the case with the present system, end up by attaining none of them.

A more productive line of thinking, therefore, might be to explore how far these goals might be made compatible with one another. It might be argued, for example, that the best way to promote the economic health of society might be to assist as many people as possible to a high level of autonomous thinking, since, among other things, this might well increase their levels of creativity and adaptability and thus enable them to make a more valuable contribution to economic productivity. If this were so, our educational provision could be tailored towards individual development in the confident knowledge that that is also the route to economic success. This, however, requires a level of sophistication which we are still some way from and which, it seems, our major economic rivals, most notably Japan, are just coming to.

The third general point worth noting is the confusion that is often to be seen between rhetoric and reality in discussions of educational policies, and the consequent need to be constantly vigilant in order to distinguish these. Quite often we are offered educational prescriptions and policies framed in terms of one kind of rationale when, on closer examination, it becomes quite clear that their real rationale is very different. The most common example of this is the dressing up of what are at root economically focused policies in the trappings, and with the rhetoric, of education for personal fulfilment: proposals, for example, for technologically orientated curricula supported by extremely questionable arguments concerning the need for everyone to come to terms with living in a technological society. The history of education, here and elsewhere, is littered with examples of attempts thus to sugar what might otherwise be seen as unpalatable pills, to win acceptance for policies which, if not so concealed, might prove unacceptable. Plato, it will be remembered, went so far as to invent a 'magnificent myth' concerning the different metals each person has within his or her constitution from birth and the different kinds of education, and also status in society, to which all are consequently, and indisputably, to be assigned. The rhetoric of the 1988 Act emphasizes 'reform', the 'raising of standards' and 'spiritual, moral, cultural, mental and physical development' (1988 Act, s. 1(2)); later chapters may show how far this is matched by the realities – even of its intentions.

The reference to Plato's 'magnificent myth' takes us naturally to a further dimension of this debate about the goals and purposes of the education system: the relationship between education and social equality.

EDUCATION AND EQUALITY

Within the context of state-provided education, there has run across this debate about the goals and purposes of education another thread, providing the woof to its warp, that of equality of educational opportunity. For, especially if one takes the view that education is access to that which is worthwhile in the culture or an opportunity to develop one's intellect and extend one's scope, it becomes a major further issue whether such access or such opportunity should be made available to all pupils or only to a privileged few, whether, if the state is to finance educational provision, it should do so for the advantage of all children or only for those who will offer it some return for its investment. It would be wrong, therefore, not to consider here this dimension of the debate about education, and

Parental Choice

indeed of the historical development of the education system in the United Kingdom.

There is nothing that requires us, whatever view of education we embrace, to advocate that that form of education should be made available to everyone. Indeed, some of the views we have considered are such as to render education, as some of those views define it, inaccessible to many pupils, as Plato made very clear. If, for example, education really is initiation into 'the best that has been thought and said', and this is interpreted, as once it was, as Classical literature, or even if it is interpreted in a more contemporary way as science, mathematics, foreign literature, English literature and so on, it is quite clear that, for a variety of reasons, many pupils will be incapable of pursuing this form of education to any significant degree, even if they are willing to. Thus, on this kind of definition, education is not for everyone but only for those capable of coping with it.

It will be clear too that, if one's view of education is that its prime purpose is economic productivity, there will be no parallel requirement that it should offer anything to those members of society with little or nothing to contribute to that economic productivity. Hence there was no attempt to offer the masses any form of education when this was not necessary for the nation's economy. Hence too, even when education for all became an economic and industrial necessity, for many people it meant little more than selecting for educational provision those pupils, regardless of their social origins, who seemed to display talents that might be cultivated to the nation's economic advantage. This attitude also explains that parallel concern with using education to bring children up to an acceptance of the political status quo and of their own lot in society. To develop the talents of those who can contribute to society's advancement and to 'gentle' the rest has long been a popular philosophy at many levels of the educational debate, but especially of course at the political level.

It is this that has bedevilled attempts to clarify the issue of equality in education or, rather, that has led to the emergence of two quite different theories of equality or versions of the equality principle. The first of these is concerned merely with equality of opportunity or, as it is often now expressed, equality of access. This was once described as the 'strong' or 'meritocratic' principle (Crosland, 1961). It is essentially the view of Plato, which we noted earlier. It is a view which contends that there are certain superior forms of human activity, a 'high culture', for the most part intellectual, and these require a high level of intellectual capability; if education is initiation into these, then, on this version of the equality principle, we need do no more than identify those pupils, whatever their social or ethnic origins, who are capable of being so initiated and ensure that they have help and support in developing their intellectual capacities for these purposes. The economic version of this principle is that we identify all the pupils who show capability in those areas of human activity

Ed ✓ Training

deemed to be economically useful and give them every help and support to develop those capabilities.

This version of the equality principle does not require of us that we do anything with or for those pupils who do not reveal these potentialities. They can be offered something different, inferior, something which on this definition is not education. If they are incapable of taking advantage of the opportunities given them to go to grammar schools, into higher education, to reach the designated attainment targets ahead of their fellows, they can be offered something else, or even nothing else: to continue in their elementary schools, to attend a secondary modern school, to experience a watered-down curriculum, to follow a course of overtly vocational training. It has never been clear, however, how these experiences were supposed to constitute an *education*. Indeed, on this view of the equality principle, there is no reason why they should. Once opportunities for access have been provided, its demands have been met in full. In fact, what this amounts to is the adoption of different views or concepts of education for different groups of children. This is why it is difficult to understand why this view of educational equality, as equality of access only, seems to have been from the beginning, and indeed continues to be, the view favoured by the Labour Party.

Another version of this kind of view is that offered, or at least taken, by those whom Denis Lawton (1988) has called the 'minimalists'. Their policy is that 'the state should pay for basic provision (as cheaply as possible) and parents would have the right and privilege of buying additional extras or of opting out of the system altogether' (Lawton, 1988, p. 17). He points out that this is what led Tawney (1921) to criticize 'a system run by those who felt that it was not good enough for their own children' (ibid.), and, among other examples, he offers city technology colleges as illustrative of this approach. He goes on to say: 'Minimalists are not in favour of a common curriculum, but they may advocate a low-level basic national curriculum enforced by tests' (ibid.). In this connection, we may note again the exclusion of CTCs and public schools from the requirements of the National Curriculum.

The second view of educational equality has been described as the 'weak' or 'democratic' view (Crosland, 1961). This view contends that every child is entitled to the fullest educational provision from which he or she is capable of profiting. On this view, educational provision is not to be tailored to economic productivity or even to high intellectual potential. Those children whose potential contribution to society seems minimal are regarded none the less as having the same entitlement to education as any others. Indeed, it has been argued that societies are to be judged by the way in which they treat their non-productive members, those who are limited or disadvantaged in some way. In primitive societies the economic structure does not permit of much scope in this area; some have even been known to eliminate such people, especially through forms of infanticide. It is claimed, however, that the economy of an advanced society, or one that wishes to regard itself as advanced, should make possible a more generous and humane treatment of all such members. This view of educational equality represents the application of that general social philosophy to the field of educational provision. Its watchword is entitlement. And by this it means more than entitlement to access; it means entitlement to full and appropriate provision.

It will be clear, however, that such a view requires that we rethink our notion of education; indeed, it pushes us towards that developmental view we considered earlier. For by definition this is a view which must go beyond economic considerations; it must also go beyond the notion of socialization; and it cannot embrace a view of education as initiation into activities of a kind such pupils, again by definition, cannot or will not cope with. What it must advocate, therefore, is that every child must have every opportunity to develop as a fully human, autonomous being, and that society must make the resources available for this to be possible.

Such a view requires that we adopt not only a wider concept of equality but also a concept of education which goes a long way beyond definitions framed in terms of subjects and bodies of knowledge, whether these are deemed to reflect our cultural heritage or merely what is economically useful. Indeed, it is not going too far to claim that such a concept of education is a *sine qua non* of this kind of concept of equality.

The tensions between these different views of education and these conflicting concepts of equality are apparent throughout the history of state-provided education in the United Kingdom, as well as in the current policies this book is attempting to evaluate. It will be helpful, therefore, if we look briefly at some of their manifestations in the development of the educational system, especially in the years since the 1944 Education Act, whose provisions the 1988 Act replaces. It is to this that we now turn.

CONFLICTING VIEWS IN THE DEVELOPMENT OF STATE EDUCATION

It is not the intention here to engage in a detailed exploration of the history of education in the United Kingdom. What we must do, however, is identify some conflicting and often contradictory movements within that history.

First, we must recognize that, whatever the rhetoric of the politicians, the major thrust of all the main events in the development of the state-maintained education system, certainly in its early stages, has been economic rather than altruistic. State-provided education arrived only when there was a clear need for an educated, or at least trained, workforce.

We must also note that, from the outset, this economic focus was accompanied by that concern we noted earlier to 'gentle' the masses, to bring them up to an acceptance of the social order and of their place in it (Gordon and Lawton, 1978). The opportunities presented by a system of schooling designed to ensure a minimum level of literacy and numeracy in all children, as the basis for the development of the basic skills needed by industry, were seized upon to instil in all children a basic form of morality and, especially, an acceptance of authority as a means of ensuring law and order and avoiding the social and political excesses experienced in some other nations. The corollary of this, of course, is the reluctance to accept any form of education which would encourage the great mass of the people to think for themselves.

This combined view of state education as a device for promoting simultaneously both industrial training and social obedience is one of the major threads running through the development of the state system in the United Kingdom. And it continues to be both a major motivating force behind particular initiatives and an important perspective for understanding what lies behind many of these initiatives. It is one of three such influences which have been identified by Raymond Williams (1961) in his book *The Long Revolution* (he calls its advocates 'the industrial trainers'), and of the three it is undoubtedly the strongest and most effective.

A second source of influence on the education system which Williams identifies is that group he calls 'the old humanists'. These are the people who have continued to argue for that view of education as concerned to provide access to the 'high culture' of society, to promote and propagate those cultural values implicit in great art, literature and academic pursuits of all kinds, to offer initiation into 'the best that has been thought and said'. This view has thus provided a counterpoint to the more overtly utilitarian claims of those who see education as little more than industrial and social training. It has also of course provided them with a veneer to overlay and conceal the starkness of some of their policies, a rhetoric with which, as we have seen, they have so often masked the realities of their policies.

We noted earlier, however, the inadequacies which some have seen in this kind of education, especially when it has been recognized as reflecting a culture which is not that of every group in a pluralist, multicultural society, or even that of the masses towards whom the state system has been directed. Those who have seen these deficiencies have for a long time been arguing for something different, for something which might be seen as being of value to all pupils and not merely those with the ability and inclination to accept the process of being initiated into the accepted culture. These Raymond Williams (1961) has called 'the public educators', and Denis Lawton (1988) calls them 'the comprehensive planners'. They are those who claim that everyone has a right to be educated and that society has an obligation to meet that right. But they also see education as going beyond basic, or even sophisticated, forms of industrial training and even beyond access to the accepted 'high culture'. They are thus pressing on us the notion that education must be conceived in a somewhat different way. The weakness of their case has hitherto been that they have been less than clear about how education on this view should be conceived. Clearly, they have in mind something like that developmental view we discussed earlier, a view which has in recent times been supported by a good deal of conceptual clarification. But, more specifically, they have been advocating and pressing that 'democratic' form of educational equality we suggested earlier is inevitably linked to this kind of educational philosophy. Thus, although their message has often been less than clear, their pressures for equality of this wider kind have been another important influence on the development of the system.

THE YEARS FOLLOWING THE 1944 EDUCATION ACT

This view was perhaps especially important in the framing of the 1944 Education Act and in the period that followed, a period which can be said, perhaps in more than merely the constitutional sense, to have ended with the passing of the 1988 Act. For there is no doubt that the 1944 Act was an attempt to bring into being an education system which was to offer more than an industrial or social training programme, however sophisticated such a programme might be, and which was to provide genuine educational opportunities to all 'according to age, aptitude and ability'. This was an Act whose intention was to establish an education system appropriate to 'the brave new world' which was to emerge from the experiences of the Second World War, and which was to reflect those democratic principles that had gained ground during that conflagration, whose stated purpose had been to protect them. It is worth noting that it was the work of the wartime coalition government, and the influence of the Labour Party on its framing is clear.

The years since that Act have seen many attempts to implement its basically egalitarian philosophy, although, it must be said, to relatively little effect. The school leaving age for all pupils has been progressively raised from fourteen in 1944 to sixteen today; nor is there any doubt that this two-stage exercise was designed not to keep pupils 'off the streets' (or off the unemployment registers), but to offer them what it was hoped would be genuine educational opportunities. For the first stage, the raising of the leaving age to fifteen in 1947 was described by Ellen Wilkinson, then Minister of Education, as 'an act of faith rather than of judgement' – a clear indication that its thrust was not in any sense an economic one, especially since there were serious doubts as to whether the country could afford it at the time. And the further raising of the minimum leaving age to sixteen in 1972 was the result of several surveys, conducted by government committees during the 1950s and 1960s, which indicated a disturbing wastage of talent from the system through 'early leaving'; and, while this was of concern from the economic point of view, there is no doubt that it prompted a good deal of concern of a more purely educational kind.

The introduction of comprehensive secondary education and the abolition, in most areas of England and Wales, of selection procedures, especially those of the eleven-plus, the parallel development of mixed-ability groupings, the establishment of the Certificate of Secondary Education (CSE) examination and, more recently, its merger with the General Certificate of Education (GCE) to form the General Certificate of Secondary Education (GCSE), and many other structural and administrative changes of the last several decades can all be seen as attempts to implement the basic egalitarian philosophy of the 1944 Act, to create a system which would offer genuine educational opportunities to all pupils and not merely to a privileged few, whatever the source of that privilege.

Thus, although a good deal more clarification was, and still is, needed concerning the curricular implications of the view of education held by 'the public educators', there is little doubt that during this period it did begin to gain considerable strength and, if it did not oust the concern of 'the industrial trainers' with economic productivity, it certainly came to enjoy equal prominence.

This is perhaps most clearly evinced in the views expressed in 1959 by the Crowther Report (CACE, 1959). This report was concerned primarily to advise the government on the educational provision for the 15–18 year groups, that is, those pupils who were in the years immediately following the compulsory years of schooling, but, perhaps because of that, it felt it appropriate to offer some compelling and interesting thoughts on the aims and purposes of the educational system as a whole.

In a chapter entitled 'Burdens and Benefits', the report identifies two main functions of the education system, which it claims have been present throughout its existence: as a 'national investment' (CACE, 1959, p. 54), 'the need of the community to provide an adequate supply of brains and skill to sustain its economic productivity' (ibid.); and as 'the state's duty to its future citizens' (ibid.), 'the right of every boy and girl to be educated' (ibid.), a right which 'exists regardless of whether, in each individual case, there will be any return' (ibid.), as 'one of the social services of the welfare state' (ibid.).

The report goes on to say:

> In this report, we have made no attempt to disentangle these two purposes of education. Both are worthy and compelling, and we accept them both. Primacy must be given to the human rights of the individual boy and girl. But we do not believe that the pursuit of national efficiency can be ranked much lower – not least because without it the human rights themselves will not be secure.
>
> (CACE, 1959, p. 55)

Thus we can see that by 1959 considerable strides had been taken towards an official recognition of the importance of the human dimension of education and of the need to plan a system that would meet demands of this kind as well as those for economic productivity.

Much that happened in the 1960s can best be understood as part of the attempt to discover and/or create such a system. The establishment of the Schools Council in 1964 (while economic factors may have played a major part in its creation, its nature reflected the concerns we are discussing here); the focus of its work on the needs of those pupils in secondary schools who were not following traditional courses leading to GCE examinations; its concern with 'the young school leaver'; the institution of the CSE examination in response to the recommendations of the Beloe Report in 1960 (SSEC, 1960); the raising of the school leaving age to sixteen in 1972; the slow spread of comprehensive secondary education and its acceleration as a result of DES Circular 10/65; the introduction of mixed-ability groupings at all levels of schooling; these and many more such developments reflected a growing concern with the need for, and a progressive attempt to implement, an education system which would be democratic, which would meet the needs of all pupils and which would regard all their needs as equally deserving of time, attention and, above all, resources. These aims and ambitions were also expressed in two further official government reports: those of the Newsom (CACE, 1963) and Plowden (CACE, 1967) Committees.

THE RETURN TO MORE TRADITIONAL VIEWS

The early 1970s saw the beginnings of a reaction against these developments, a swing away from these more democratic views of what the education system exists to do and the reassertion of those arguments for economic value, for proper returns from the investment of public money in the education system.

In part, this can be attributed to economic recession, particularly that which followed the oil crisis of 1973–4, when the oil-producing and exporting countries (OPEC) decided to raise dramatically the price of oil. This action had an immediate impact on many aspects of the nation's economy. And, although in the event the education budget continued to expand in real terms until 1977, its implications for the education service were that less money was to be made available for its funding, that there would be increased concern to obtain 'value for money' from that funding and that there would be tighter restrictions and controls on how that money was spent.

It must be noted, however, that even before this there had been significant reactions against some of the developments which we saw just now had been prompted by the egalitarian philosophy of the 1944 Act, and particularly the attempts to implement that philosophy which had been supported and encouraged by the Crowther Report (CACE, 1959) and by those which had followed it – the

Newsom Report (CACE, 1963) on the education of the 'less able' pupil in the secondary school and the Plowden Report (CACE, 1967) on primary education, as well as the Robbins Report (CHE, 1963) on higher education. In 1969, for example, the first of a series of 'Black Papers' (Cox and Dyson, 1969a, 1969b; Cox and Boyson, 1977) had been published, a collection of papers which claimed that recent innovations, such as the replacement of grammar schools by comprehensive schools, the introduction of mixed-ability classes, the use of 'informal methods' in primary schools and changes in the ethos and value structures of universities, were leading to a serious decline in educational standards, especially apparent, they claimed (although without supporting evidence), in a fall in levels of attainment in what they called, without clear definition, 'the basic skills'. 'The old humanists' had re-emerged.

This kind of claim was reiterated at this time by the Confederation of British Industry, which also began to assert that schools were not paying enough attention to 'the basic skills' (still not clearly defined) or to applied forms of the arts and sciences. In short, not only was it now being claimed that educational standards were falling but also, and more importantly, that the economic function of education was being neglected in favour of other, less economically productive concerns. Thus 'the industrial trainers' also returned to the fray.

In 1976 this view was given overt endorsement at government level when, as Prime Minister in a Labour government, James Callaghan made a speech at Ruskin College, in which he directly attacked the teaching profession for failing to respond to the needs of the economy, in particular by encouraging pupils to study to advanced levels subjects which he deemed to be not directly productive in economic and commercial terms. Too many sixth-form pupils, he claimed, were studying arts and humanities subjects, and correspondingly too few studying science and technology. This was leading to a similar imbalance in higher education. And this unsatisfactory state of affairs was felt to be a direct result of allowing teachers too much freedom in the planning of the school curriculum. And perhaps it was an inevitable result of that policy, since most teachers make their educational decisions in the light of what they feel to be in the best interests of their pupils, what they feel may be of most value to them as persons, rather than as part of a set of policies for economic growth.

This speech is often seen as the first overt statement of this kind of government policy for education. However, at least one event of some significance in this respect had preceded it. In 1974 the Manpower Services Commission had been established with a clear brief, and corresponding resources, to develop schemes within education to correct the perceived mismatch between what schools were offering their pupils and the needs of employers. In short, machinery had been created for the funding of the education system via a new route, one which would and could ensure greater centralized control of the way in which this funding was used, and especially ensure that it would be used to support and sponsor forms of curriculum designed with economic productivity in mind. Its focus has been on the further education (16–19) sector of education, but this term has increasingly been seen as embracing the 14–18 age group, so that the impact of developments under this aegis has progressively been felt further down the schooling system. Schemes such as the Youth Opportunities Programme (YOP), the Youth Training Scheme (YTS) and the Technical and Vocational Educational Initiative (TVEI) have led to schools being funded from sources with very clear strings, of an instrumental and vocational kind, attached, and thus to a shift of emphasis within the education system back to that of 'the industrial trainers', and of the social trainers too, which we saw earlier had lost some of its strength in the years following the 1944 Act. In this connection it is worth noting that it has been made very clear that developments under the TVEI scheme are expected to continue for the fourteen-to-eighteen-year-olds in parallel with the new National Curriculum, and £900 million has been made available over the ten-year period which commenced in September 1987 to support the extension of TVEI to all maintained secondary schools and colleges (DES, 1989d).

Inevitably too, as was suggested earlier, this has led to a return to a largely élitist system, since that egalitarianism, which it was claimed is an essential part of a system of education designed to meet the needs of all pupils, must give way once new forms of selectivity, and also of competition, begin to appear. Thus the secondary modern/grammar school distinction, which comprehensivization was intended to obliterate, has been replaced by a technical–vocational/academic divide, in which those pupils in the former category again come to be given something whose justification in *educational* terms becomes very difficult to argue. The notion of *education* for all has thus been eroded; so too has the Crowther Report's view that the economic purposes of the system cannot, or should not, be given a higher priority than the social service dimension; and the idealism of the 1944 Act has given way to something which reflects little more than stark economic manipulation.

THE NATIONAL CURRICULUM IN ITS HISTORICAL CONTEXT

The last decade or so, then, has seen a number of measures designed to reassert the economic function of the education system as prime and to create a context in which teachers' natural inclinations to place the emphasis elsewhere might be controlled and inhibited. Progressive changes have been made in the methods, and indeed the scale, of funding education and educational initiatives, at all levels from the nursery to higher education, of such a kind as to encourage increased emphasis on those subjects and those areas of teaching which are regarded as being most useful to the economy, and there has been a corresponding reduction of emphasis and expenditure on other aspects of education, again at every level.

This has been accompanied by the introduction of many devices and procedures for reducing the autonomy of teachers and controlling their activities more closely, mainly to ensure that they place the emphasis where official government policy requires it to be placed and not where we have suggested they are inclined most naturally to place it – on the developmental needs of their pupils. Thus we have seen the introduction of schemes for teacher accountability and appraisal, again at all levels; enhanced powers for governing bodies; increased involvement of industry in the management of education, through greater representation on governing bodies of all kinds of educational institutions, but perhaps especially through membership of the planning committees of university institutions; pay rises linked to the acceptance of procedures and devices of this kind; direct control of the content and methods of teacher training to ensure that new teachers entering the profession do so with new attitudes and views of their role; and, in general, changes in all areas of the structure and management of the educational system designed to ensure greater external control in the interests of an increased focus on the economic and utilitarian aspects of that system.

These developments have all reached their culmination in the 1988 Education Act and the National Curriculum which is its central feature. For that Act, as we saw in Chapter 1, prescribes the subjects that must now constitute the school curriculum and their relative levels of importance in the planning of that curriculum, underlining those, such as mathematics, science, English and technology, which have clearly been selected primarily for their economic and utilitarian value. This emphasis has become very clear in the implementation of this part of the Act, as we have learned of the specification of the content of these subjects that is to be taught and the levels of attainment which it is claimed are the appropriate levels for pupils to have reached at the given key stages. Thus teachers now have little or no 'say' in what they are to teach or in what kind of curricular provision they make for their pupils; the only scope they have is in relation to the methods they will adopt to 'deliver' the content of a curriculum which has been determined elsewhere.

Furthermore, as we also saw in Chapter 1, there are to be regular checks on the attainment of all pupils, and, with the aggregation and publication of these, on the achievement of schools and teachers too. This is a deliberate move to introduce an element of commercial competition into education, and different, but parallel, measures have been introduced to extend this to higher education as well. Not only is the education system to prepare pupils for the commercial competitiveness of society at large, they must themselves become part of it.

Again, therefore, we have a device which will ensure that teachers focus their energies on raising levels of attainment in the key subjects of the National Curriculum with an inevitable emphasis on promoting the attainment of those pupils most likely to 'do them proud'. For future funding, and perhaps even survival, may well depend on the aggregated test results and on the responses of the public and the politicians to these. Thus schools and other educational institutions will not merely have a duty to promote economic awareness and to enhance the nation's economic growth; they will also have to enter into the market-place and themselves become commercially competitive. This is the thrust, the intention as well as the effect, of those provisions of the Act, which we also noted in Chapter 1, for 'opting out' and applying for direct funding from the Secretary of State, and for seeking establishment as a city technology college with funding, at least in part, from any industrial or commercial organization willing to provide such funding.

The 1988 Act, then, can be seen to encapsulate and to codify in the statute book all those developments which over the last decade or so have been taking the education system back to a utilitarian philosophy, to an emphasis on economic success, to the ideology of 'the industrial trainers', and thus away from the philosophy of 'the public educators', from the 'weak' or 'democratic' notion of equality, from the Crowther Report's view of education as one of the social services of the welfare state and from the 1944 Act's promise of 'education for all according to age, aptitude and ability'.

Subsequent chapters will endeavour to identify some of the implications and ramifications of this highly significant shift of focus.

SUMMARY AND CONCLUSIONS

This chapter has set out to show, first, that a number of different views can be held about the goals and purposes of education and of any education system, and that, second, these several different views can all be discerned competing for dominance in the development of the education system in the United Kingdom. In particular, it has identified a continuing and perhaps irreconcilable conflict between the view of education as a right that should be safeguarded for every person in any society which claims to be advanced, or even civilized, and that of education as primarily concerned to promote economic success.

The chapter went on to claim that the 1944 Education Act represented an attempt to create a legislative context in which both these purposes might be met, and that for twenty years or so after that Act had been passed every effort was made to achieve this, to create an egalitarian system which would offer to all pupils an educational experience which might be of value to them as individuals as well as assisting society to meet the demands of economic health and productivity.

It concluded by tracing the stages in a return to policies of a more overtly utilitarian kind, prompted by a sense that the emphasis had swung too far in the opposite direction, and attempted to show how these have culminated in the 1988 Act, whose flavour is essentially that of a manifesto for 'value for money', for competitive commercialism, for the élitism which must follow from such competitiveness and for a return to the values and standards of a commercially orientated system of education at every level.

Our next chapter will endeavour to unpack some of the theoretical issues touched upon here more explicitly in order to evaluate them more fully.

3

THE NATIONAL CURRICULUM – A CONCEPTUAL EVALUATION

The introduction to this book stressed the inadequacy, indeed the dangers, of a view of evaluation which requires us to wait until the year 2000, when the first group of pupils to experience all eleven years of the National Curriculum will emerge, before we attempt an assessment of its success or failure, its merits and its drawbacks, its pluses and its minuses. Such a policy would encourage us to see evaluation as limited to an assessment of the outcomes of this curriculum or, even more narrowly, to an appraisal of the extent to which it had been successfully 'delivered'. There is far more to curriculum evaluation than that, as the introduction suggested.

Developments in evaluation theory in recent years have shown the evaluative process within education to be a highly complex and sophisticated matter. They have, among other things, revealed the need for evaluation to be seen as part of the process of curriculum change and/or development from the very outset. And so they have stressed the value of *formative* evaluation in contrast to that which is merely *summative*, the merits of making continuous assessments of all educational practices (much in the way that all successful teachers do in relation to the development of their own professional work), in order to ensure constant feedback of understandings to inform the process of revising, modifying, adapting and, indeed, restructuring the original plans to reflect the experience of attempting to implement them. Such a process will be difficult to maintain in the context of policies which allow little scope for revision, modification, adaptation or restructuring, except possibly at the national level; but that should not deter us from undertaking such evaluation, since, whether things can be changed or not, it is important to be in a position to make an informed judgement about them. And there are suggestions in the reports of the subject working groups that modifications will be needed in the light of experience, the implication of this being that some form of formative evaluation will be necessary. Professor Cox, for example, in forwarding to the Secretary of State the report of the English Working Group, says in his covering letter, 'We also emphasize that our recommendations have to be proved in the classroom, and may in due course need to be revised following careful evaluation of the results.'

This, however, raises questions of what we may mean by 'results' and how wide the 'careful evaluation' of these is to be. And it takes us on to a second major point: for a second important feature of evaluation theory, as it has developed over the last few decades, is the awareness that there are two significant, but quite distinct, dimensions to curriculum evaluation. There is the *empirical* evaluation of the effects of a particular form of curriculum, or, again more narrowly, of the success with which it has been implemented or 'delivered' – a kind of 'consumer research' activity. There is also, however, what has been called the *conceptual* or *value* dimension of curriculum evaluation (White, 1971), a form of evaluation which concerns itself not with questions of empirical 'fact' concerning the implementation or 'delivery' of the curriculum, but with questions of judgement concerning its worth or its value, and, beyond this, one must now add, the way in which it has been conceptualized: not 'Is the curriculum being "delivered" effectively?', or even 'Does it have any side effects?', but 'Is this curriculum worth "delivering"?' and, further, 'Is it conceptually sound?' Clearly, these last are forms of evaluation which can, and should be, undertaken not only during but even before *any* attempt at curriculum change, certainly before one as dramatic and as sweeping as the introduction of a national curriculum. It is this kind of evaluation which will be the focus of this chapter.

To make such a conceptual evaluation, however, requires far more than that we say whether we like the curriculum or not. It requires at the very least that we make clear why we approve or disapprove, what our judgement is based on. And, in order to make that clear, we need to know in some depth what it is we are making a judgement about and, at this stage in our discussion of the National Curriculum, that is far from apparent. In short, a conceptual judgement or evaluation requires a conceptual analysis of what is being judged or evaluated as a basis for a clear understanding both of what in essence it is and, consequently, of what features of it we like or dislike, accept or reject, approve or disapprove.

It is this kind of conceptual analysis which this chapter will undertake. To do so will necessitate considering three major issues, addressing three major questions. First, we need to try to get to grips with the underlying rationale of the National Curriculum, its implicit ideology. Second, we must make some evaluation of that rationale or ideology. This will not mean declaring it to be good or bad, right or wrong, or even indifferent, since those are matters of judgement, and expressions of our own preferences or predilections cannot be part of any attempt at objective evaluation. What is necessary is that we attempt some exploration of the National Curriculum's own value system and its conceptual structure in order to ascertain whether these are clear, and, further, whether they are internally coherent and consistent, whether the reality matches the rhetoric. For on that issue we may be able to make an objective judgement: not 'Do we like it?' but, to put it simply, 'Does it make overall sense?' And, third, as part of that exploration, we need to evaluate it against a range of conceptual understandings of curriculum and of curriculum planning available to us from recent studies in the field, to discover how far, if at all, the National Curriculum reflects those understandings or takes account of them. For, again, it is legitimate to ask, and it is possible to answer objectively, the question whether at the conceptual level it recognizes or ignores, whether it is consistent or inconsistent with current understandings of such matters as the existence of different concepts of curriculum, of education, of equality and, indeed, of childhood, different approaches to curriculum planning, the role of subjects and of knowledge in the educational process and many more.

In short, we need to undertake a proper conceptual analysis of the National Curriculum not merely to make our own judgements about its value but also, and more importantly, to make a sound evaluation of its conceptual structure. We *do* need to ask ourselves whether we like or approve of this form of curriculum, but to answer that question we need a clearer understanding of what form of curriculum it is. And, beyond that, we need to evaluate it in terms of its conceptual underpinning or framework, to decide whether that is as sound as it might be. We need to ask whether it has taken advantage of what we know and understand about educational planning. For we need to make a judgement about its own intellectual quality. If my dentist pulls out all my teeth and fits dentures merely because he or she is ignorant of the latest developments in dental science, I can evaluate his or her practice not merely by asserting that I, personally, do not like it (for that would appear a somewhat biased judgement), but also, and objectively, in terms of its lack of awareness of current knowledge, or even merely of current understandings. In this respect educational provision is no different. And its quality needs to be judged in the same way, by reference to its level of conceptual sophistication.

Before we can embark on making that kind of judgement, however, we need to be clear about the conceptual underpinning of the National Curriculum.

THE IMPLICIT IDEOLOGY OF THE NATIONAL CURRICULUM

It may be worth noting first of all that the 1988 Education Act is the first such Act to offer no statement of its philosophy or its underlying ideals, beyond the rather bland claim that its concern is to raise educational standards; a claim which, as we shall see later, is not very helpful since it is accompanied by no definition of what it takes educational standards to be. Thus, in order to evaluate its philosophy, one needs first to identify the values implicit in its provisions, the main general features of its value structure.

There would seem to be at least three major features of the rationale, or ideology, of the National Curriculum and its attendant legislation which one can identify: its instrumentalism, its commercialism and its consequent élitism. We saw enough in Chapter 2 to know that a view of education which displays these features is perfectly legitimate. It is important, however, to recognize that it is this kind of view that current policies reflect and are concerned to implement. It will be worth looking at each in turn – not least in order to be clear that these really do constitute the underlying philosophy of the Act.

Instrumentalism

It would seem quite clear that the 1988 Act, and especially the National Curriculum, have been framed by people whose view of schooling is from the outside and whose prime concern is with what education is *for* rather than with what it *is*. In fact, there is little evidence that its architects understand the second of these concepts. For, in addition to embracing a view of education as concerned entirely with the attainment of certain, clearly prespecified objectives (an issue we will return to in a later section), it makes it quite clear that its central concern is 'to secure for all pupils in maintained schools a curriculum which equips them with the knowledge, skills and understanding that they need for adult life and employment' (DES, 1987, p. 3). This intention, as we saw in Chapter 1, is reasserted in greater detail in the Act itself. There is thus a clear indication here that educational provision is to be planned according to the needs of adulthood rather than of childhood, that childhood is conceived as a period of preparation for what is to follow.

Furthermore, that this instrumentalism is at base prompted by economic considerations is also clear. In the same section of the 'consultation' document, for example, we read not only that we must 'raise standards consistently' but also, and further, that we must raise them 'at least as quickly as they are rising in competitor countries' (ibid.). There is little doubt that the selection of the core subjects within the National Curriculum is directed at achieving the same economic ends. It is difficult to argue on any other grounds for the superiority of scientific or mathematical studies over the historical or the artistic. Nor is this view of the National Curriculum dispelled by an examination of the detailed analyses of individual subjects which, as again we saw in Chapter 1, have been undertaken subsequent to the passing of the Act.

Thus we must note the loss, if not the positive rejection, of the notion that education may be, perhaps should be, concerned with study for study's sake, with the pursuit of knowledge whose value may be claimed to be in some way intrinsic, that, for example, the *main* concern of the study of 'English' might be to develop literary appreciation – coupled with that enhancement of the individual's intellectual powers and capacities which language development can bring – rather than to ease commercial transactions or ensure quality of business correspondence. The report of the English Working Group does of course discuss and recommend the former view of the teaching of English; but its proposed attainment targets and profile components, as we saw in Chapter 1, appear to place the main emphasis on the latter.

It seems clear that, as was suggested in Chapter 2, the dominant view is now that of Raymond Williams's (1961) 'industrial trainers' and that, in relation to primary education, the pre-eminent tradition is now the 'preparatory' rather than the 'developmental' (Blyth, 1965), that which again sees the experiences of pupils in the primary phase in relation to what these are preparing them *for* rather than in terms of any intrinsic, or developmental, value they might have.

The concept of vocationalism implicit in these policies is also a narrow, simplistic and instrumental one. There is no doubt that schooling must be concerned with vocational preparation, but, apart from the dangers of seeing this as its sole concern, there is also the issue of what we mean by vocationalism, and there is a strong case for claiming that a simplistic, instrumental view of vocational training is inappropriate for an advanced and rapidly changing economy. Again, the Crowther Report was interesting and perceptive in its comments on this issue, suggesting that in a time of rapid technological change 'the first quality that is needed to cope with such a world is adaptability' (CACE, 1959, p. 52). It went on to say that 'this need for adaptability exposes an ambiguity in the word "skill" ' (ibid.), and that 'it may be that there will even be a reduced need in the future for "skill" in the old-fashioned sense of the term: what will be needed in ever growing volume will be the quality that can best be described as "general mechanical intelligence" ' (op. cit., p. 53). Thirty years later we can add that the development of such a quality requires a curriculum that emphasizes the processes of learning rather than its content or its objectives – a point we shall return to later in this chapter.

The idea that, even in relation to its economic and vocational functions, education should be concerned to promote adaptability and flexibility remains a very powerful idea; indeed, technological development since the 1950s may well have increased its significance. Certainly, many of those best placed to advise us on what is needed for economic success have stressed its importance. James Pilditch (1987), for example, in a book designed to inform us 'how "winning" companies create the products we all want to buy', recommends not a narrowly conceived and tightly controlled form of vocational education but advises us rather to 'welcome chaos and creativity'; he quotes Marshall McLuhan as saying that 'ideas have become the main ingredient of the new economy', and Edward de Bono as claiming that 'the quality of our future depends on the quality of our thinking' (Pilditch, 1987, p. 149). He is then explicitly critical of current educational practices: 'all our education prompts us to suppress imagination. The logical, numerate, literate, educated mind can kill ideas before they start' (ibid.), and 'many formally educated people . . . have their imagination ironed out of them' (op. cit., pp. 149–50). One also notes that our major 'competitor countries', most notably Japan and West Germany, but also Sweden and even the USSR, are for these reasons moving away from the rigidities of their national curricula.

In spite of this, the newly devised National Curriculum in the United Kingdom emphasizes an instrumental view of schooling, exercises a tight control of the content of the curriculum and repeats what, as long as twenty years ago, was dubbed the 'vocational fallacy'.

We must, therefore, both recognize the instrumentalism of current policies and note some of the inadequacies of this approach even within the narrow field of economic and vocational aspects of schooling. The recognition of this takes us naturally on to the second main feature of these policies we noted earlier: their commercialism.

Commercialism

It is perhaps worth noting first the commercial imagery that is a feature of much of the 1988 Act's supporting documentation. We read of the 'providers' of education, of the 'delivery' of the curriculum, of 'machinery' for accomplishing this and that, of the 'users' of the system, of its 'consumers', of our 'competitors', and so on. The picture is that of a factory-farming approach to schooling. Elliot Eisner (1985) has summed this up very well in his description of the 'job analysis' approach to educational planning which began to be favoured in the early part of this century:

> The school was seen as a *plant*. The *superintendent* directed the operation of the plant. The teachers were engaged in a job of *engineering*, and the pupils were the *raw material* to be processed in that plant according to the demands of the *consumers*. Furthermore, the product was to be judged at regular intervals along the production line using *quality control standards* which were to be quantified to reduce the likelihood of error. *Product specifications* were to be prescribed before the raw material was processed. In this way efficiency, measured with respect to cost primarily, could be determined.
>
> (Eisner, 1985, p. 42)

Imagery, or metaphor, need not necessarily of course match reality, but, as Eisner points out elsewhere (1982, p. 6), metaphors 'shape our conception of the problems we study' and, we might add in this context, they also reflect the values and the attitudes of those using them.

That the commercial metaphor reflects the values and attitudes of the architects of current policies is clear from those policies themselves. We have only to note the emphasis that recent years have seen on school management – as opposed to *curriculum* management – and on the training of headteachers as managers. We noted in Chapter 1 how important an aspect of current policies is the notion of local financial management of schools. And we must recognize the commercial competitiveness which is the essential concomitant of the publication of test results and the inevitable and consequential drawing up of 'league tables'. Such tables have already appeared in the press in relation to the relative research records of university institutions, and these records are being used as the basis for determining appropriate levels of funding. Furthermore, the funding of university institutions is already at a level which makes their survival dependent on securing external, mainly commercial, finance and on their success in competing with one another for student enrolments. This will also be the effect of the publication of aggregated test results by schools. Thus these policies reflect the complete commercialization of education from the nursery to the university, the application to education of the Thatcherite policy of self-help, value for money and survival of the fittest – education as a national investment *par excellence*.

Furthermore, the privatization of all the major utilities in society is matched in education by those opportunities for 'opting out' and the invitation to establish commercially funded city technology colleges which we noted in Chapter 1, just as attempts are currently being made to replace large segments of the National Health Service with private medical schemes. Privatization is a current watchword; and there is a clear conceptual link between privatization and commercialism.

It is far from self-evident, however, that commercial competition is either appropriate to a professional activity such as education, or medicine, or conducive to increased quality of provision in fields of this kind. For it must introduce extraneous, strictly irrelevant, and in some contexts even dangerous, considerations into the minds of those who plan and practise in these areas. One does from time to time, for example, read in the press of dentists who have filled or capped excessive numbers of their patients' teeth. The profit motive is not appropriate in professional contexts, and commercial competitiveness must cloud professional judgement, the essence and prime motive of which is, or ought to be, a concern with the needs of the client (rather than the 'consumer'). A high score in the national testing programme, or a high place in a 'league table', need not reflect that a school is doing its best for all its pupils, although it may indicate that it is doing its best to respond to the targets set for the supposed economic and commercial needs of society. In this connection it is worth remembering that the

first acknowledged great educational practitioner of the Western world was So-
crates, whose policy of constant questioning was directed primarily at that group
of people known as the sophists, who sold education for profit, taught 'useful
skills' and offered clear-cut answers even to the most intractable questions, in
order to maximize that profit and, in pursuit of the same goal, were by no means
reluctant to offer adulterated wares. And, while visiting the classical world, we
might also note the assertion of Seneca: 'I respect no study and deem no study
good which results in money-making.'

One does not wish to appear to be arguing that schools do not share a responsibility for the future of society. As David Aspin (1981, p. 44) has said, in
commenting on *The School Curriculum* (DES, 1981), 'it would be a brave man
who would agree that we should "take no thought for the morrow"; but this
document seems to be almost entirely devoted to the cares of the morrow rather
than the possibilities of the present'.

One consequence of this commercialism, allied to the instrumentalism we
noted earlier, is its implications for the quality of life in our society, what Edward
Heath, in commenting on the Act, referred to as its 'philistinism'. Enoch Powell
(1985), as we saw in Chapter 2, has also attacked this kind of utilitarianism as
leading to what he has called a 'modern barbarism'. Both have been concerned to
highlight the unsatisfactory features of a society which places all its emphasis on
the *means* to economic productivity with little or no concern for the *ends* these
serve, or might serve, or to the quality of life such economic productivity might
make possible. This is brought out particularly well in that saying of Confucius to
which I constantly make reference: 'If you have two pence to spend, you should
spend one penny on bread and one penny on a flower – the bread to make life
possible, the flower to make it worthwhile.' And, in the context of education, we
might quote the Newsom Report (CACE, 1963, p. 117): 'An education that
makes complete sense must provide opportunity for personal fulfilment – for the
good life as well as for good living.' And we may note David Aspin's further
comment (Aspin, 1981, p. 44) on *The School Curriculum* (DES, 1981), that 'both
parents and employers would broadly agree that what matters to people in the last
analysis is that they can look forward to a life *of some quality*'.

Finally, on this point, we may note the words of Tony Benn, who, in a recent
speech, criticized both major parties for failing to raise or address questions
about the kind of society we wish to see: 'While we go on worshipping profit and
neglecting need, prattling endlessly about productivity, competitiveness and economic efficiency, we are missing the central question, which is whether we want
to be a community of interdependent people or driven back to the jungle where
the strongest devour the weakest.'

This quotation raises a further aspect of the commercialism of current policies
which takes us on to the third and last major feature we identified at the start of

this section – their élitism. For élitism is a *sine qua non* of competitive commercialism, which has little point if it is not concerned centrally, as Benn's words imply, with the survival of the fittest.

Élitism

It was suggested in Chapter 2 that the 1988 Act has replaced the egalitarian philosophy of the 1944 Act with something which rejects the ideals which lay behind that Act – perhaps because of our failure in forty years to attain them – and propounds a very different set of values. To put it into the terminology we used there, it has adopted a 'strong' or 'meritocratic' version of the equality principle, as equality of access, and rejected the 'weak', 'democratic' version of 'education for all according to age, aptitude and ability'. We gave some reasons in Chapter 2 for making this claim. In the light of our earlier discussion in this chapter, we can now add to those.

The emphasis on economic productivity and competitive commercialism reflects a move away from the social service function of education toward the view that educational provision is justified mainly, if not entirely, as a 'national investment'. For economic productivity will not be served by the expenditure of relatively scarce resources on pupils who demonstrate that they have little to contribute to it. And this some pupils will demonstrate at a very early age and stage through the national testing programme. Furthermore, the invitation to, or even the obligation on, schools to compete with one another in these testing exercises is counterproductive to any notion that they exist to serve the needs of all their pupils equally. Properly competitive farmers do not feed up the runts of any litter; they certainly do not offer them the same level of care and provision they give to the sturdy products. To do so would be to reveal a lack of appreciation of the realities of what commercialism implies. There is an empirical point here, which we must take up in Chapter 4 in relation to what we know of the actual effects on schools, teachers, pupils and, indeed, parents of the old 11+ selection tests; but there is a logical, conceptual point too. The concept of equality of treatment is not compatible with that of competition. This, after all, is the nub of the socialism versus capitalism debate.

One could of course argue that it is possible for a society to promote commercial competitiveness in the pursuit of wealth and economic success and to use some of that wealth and economic success deliberately to support the welfare of its less favoured citizens. Indeed, it might be argued, as we noted in Chapter 2, that the quality of a society is to be judged, at least in part, by how it treats its less favoured members, those whose contribution to its economic health may be minimal or even non-existent. However, it has to be pointed out that in such a society the social services themselves would not be forced into a competitive mould, nor would their levels of funding be progressively reduced in parallel with a reduction in taxation. The fact that education has been so treated is clear evidence of the fundamental élitism of these policies and of the National Curriculum as a major feature of them.

Élitism is also an inevitable result of any curriculum which, like the National Curriculum, is subject-based, defined in terms of the subjects which must be taught and the conceptions of these subjects as set out in profile components, attainment targets and programmes of study. Again, this is in part an empirical point which we will take up in Chapter 5, since there is much evidence that the selection of subjects and of subject content by reference to the intentions of the curriculum planners rather than to the pupils who are the recipients of the curriculum leads to rejection and failure, usually attributable to factors such as class, race and also gender. Again, however, the point to be made here is the conceptual point that a common curriculum framed in terms of subjects and their content must reflect the value system of those who so frame it and cannot, therefore, reflect the value systems of the many different groups, social and ethnic, in society whose needs it is supposed to meet. This it can only do, as we shall see later, if it is framed in terms of something like the 'areas of experience' which an earlier, and apparently quickly outmoded, document from Her Majesty's Inspectorate identified in listing the 'eight adjectives' which delineate these several areas: aesthetic/creative, ethical, linguistic, mathematical, physical, scientific, social/political and spiritual (DES, 1977), a list to which was later added 'technological'. This statement, as we shall see in Chapter 6, led to the emergence of the notion of the 'entitlement curriculum' which was, quite properly and reasonably, defined in these terms. This kind of loose definition is the only kind which can ensure both equality and minimal levels of provision. However, it leads also to a less tight form of central control of the curriculum, since it necessitates the making of professional judgements by teachers in relation to the requirements of their individual pupils. It means, as Lord Joseph put it in the House of Lords in criticizing the rigidity of the National Curriculum, that schools and local authorities should be required only to 'have regard to' the demands of the National Curriculum and that the detailed interpretation of those demands must be left to the teachers' professional judgement. But of course that would mean that teachers would be likely to continue to place more emphasis on what they see as the interests of their pupils and less on the economic needs of society than is currently wanted. The converse, then, is what now holds: that converse, because of its rigid subject and content base, is inflexibly élitist.

This élitism which results from the subject-content base of the National Curriculum is exacerbated by the testing programme which is an essential part of it. Again in the Lords debate, Baroness David described this as 'selection by the back door'. And Lord Joseph also claimed that the National Curriculum would not meet the needs of non-academic pupils. This reinforces the point made earlier about the effects of competitive commercialism on educational provision.

These, then, are the major features of the underpinning philosophy of the National Curriculum and its associated policies. The analysis and critique which have just been offered will be dismissed, as they have been in other contexts, by some proponents of these policies as biased and partial, and even as distorting what the Act sets out to do and does. They will point to all the assertions in the Act and its supporting documentation which claim the opposite of what is being suggested here, which speak of education as the development of the individual, which stress the development of all pupils, and so on. Nor is there any lack of such examples and quotations in that literature.

It is for this reason that we must now turn to the second major issue which we expressed earlier the intention of exploring: that of the coherence of the value assertions and the concepts which the documentation uses. We must attempt to separate the reality from the rhetoric. We must look at the claims made in the context of the actualities of the provision and of the practice of implementation. We must examine the concepts used and ask if they are compatible with one another. We must consider whether the policies are coherent, and, if they are, of what that coherence consists, what it is that holds these policies together. Or perhaps we will have to note that the concepts used lack coherence, that it is not conceptually possible to promote individual development and economic productivity at the same time, and that, if one is claiming to do so, one is either grossly mistaken and ill informed, or one is attempting to wrap the realities of the one in the rhetoric of the other. Whatever is the case, a good deal of conceptual unpacking is necessary.

THE CONCEPTUAL BASE OF THE NATIONAL CURRICULUM

The first thing to be said about the conceptual base of the National Curriculum, in respect of its delineation in the 1988 Act and, more especially, in all the documentation which has emerged from the DES, from NCC and from SEAC in support of it, is that it reveals a disturbing lack of conceptual clarity. As John White (1988, p. 116) has said, 'the logical gaps in its argument at point after point are glaring and distressing'.

We must note this lack of clarity first of all in respect of what might be regarded as the fundamental concepts of the National Curriculum: its stated aims and purposes. First, we have been informed throughout the build-up to its introduction that its central concern and prime purpose are to raise 'standards': 'standards of attainment must be raised throughout England and Wales' (DES, 1987, p. 3). 'Standards' is a highly problematic concept which can bear many different interpretations. Yet at no stage is any attempt made to define those 'standards' with which the National Curriculum is to be concerned. The meaning given to 'standards' becomes plain when we see through the later specification of attainment targets what is meant by 'attainment'; from this, we can divine which 'standards of attainment' are to be raised: standards of attainment in the knowledge, skills and understanding related to the chosen subjects and defined by the attainment targets. We are, however, here as in many other places, left to work this out for ourselves, to divine what we are to take 'standards' to mean by an analysis of the scheme as a whole. And at no stage are we encouraged to recognize nor are we reminded that 'standards' could mean many other things, and could be defined in many other ways, not least those related to a concept of education as the development of individual potential and capacities and powers of self-determination. It also begins to appear, therefore, that this kind of interpretation of 'standards', the concept of 'standards' as the term is used within the National Curriculum, may be at odds with, and incoherent with, other concepts such as 'development' and 'potential' which the documentation also uses.

Similarly, we are offered no clear definition of a second major concept, or pair of related concepts, which is or are central to the National Curriculum. The Act itself begins by telling us, in section 2(2), that a school's curriculum will satisfy its requirements only if it is 'balanced and broadly based'. Again, we must note that the concept of balance in relation to education has been debated since the time of Plato (he called it 'harmony'), and that it has long been recognized as a highly problematic issue (Kelly, 1982, 1986, 1989). Again, it is a concept which is clearly open to many different interpretations and meanings. For Plato, the issues were those of balance between intellectual and physical development, and between the intellect and the emotions. More recently, there has been an ongoing debate about balance within the curriculum between arts and sciences, a debate which was brought into the public forum by C. P. Snow's publication in 1959 of *The Two Cultures*. And many other interpretations have been offered of what 'balance' or 'breadth' might mean in an educational context, and indeed clear statements of the fact that they are concepts which can be viewed from many different perspectives – balance of subjects, of disciplines, of content, of approaches, of experiences, of breadth and depth of study, of the cognitive and the affective, of education and vocational training.

There is also no awareness or acknowledgement that, as Helen Simons (1988, p. 82) has claimed, 'twenty-five years of curriculum review, innovation, and development have also taught us another lesson that the Government chooses to ignore . . . This is that "breadth and balance", so regularly intoned by ministers in justification of the foundation curriculum, is far less a function of subject structure than it is of how individual subjects are conceived and taught.' To this one would add that both 'breadth' and 'balance' are to be sought in the pupil's response to what is offered, to the curriculum which is *received*, rather than in the list of subjects included in the *official* curriculum provided.

Indeed, so many different interpretations of 'breadth' and 'balance' have been shown to be possible that their value as concepts within educational theory and/or planning has been seriously challenged (Kelly, 1986). At the very least, these complexities render it necessary, if the terms are to be used, that their use be accompanied by a very clear statement of how they are to be understood in any given context. Neither the 1988 Act nor its documentation, however, offers such a statement or indicates in any way an awareness of these conceptual problems and complications.

Section 2(2) of the Act does go on to offer what might be claimed to be its definition of 'a balanced and broadly based curriculum', as one which:

(a) promotes the spiritual, moral, cultural, mental and physical development of pupils . . .; and
(b) prepares such pupils for the opportunities, responsibilities and experiences of adult life.

But this definition, if definition it be, serves only to increase the confusion since it introduces several other concepts of an equally problematic kind.

Again, therefore, we are left to divine for ourselves the definition of 'balanced and broadly based' which the Act has adopted or assumed. And again we can only do this by interpreting the concrete proposals which follow and which have subsequently emerged. These make it clear that the concept of balance within the National Curriculum is the simplistic concept of a balance of subjects and subject content. We must note too, however, the difficulty of recognizing the coherence of any notion of 'breadth' or 'balance', even one framed in terms of subjects, within a curriculum which devotes 'the majority of curriculum time at primary level . . . to the [three] core subjects' (DES, 1987, p. 6) – English, mathematics and science – and '30–40 per cent of time at secondary level' (ibid.).

It is also worth noting that although a broad and balanced curriculum is thus defined in terms of its component subjects, 'the principle that each pupil should have a broad and balanced curriculum which is also relevant to his or her particular needs is now established by law' (DES, 1989c, para. 2.2). It is difficult to see how any law can resolve the logical and conceptual incompatibility and incoherence of the concepts of subject balance and relevance to individual needs.

Thus, in relation to these two major concepts of the National Curriculum, those of 'standards' and 'balance and breadth', we must note a lack of clarity, an absence of any awareness of the problematic nature of these concepts and an endemic incoherence between the meanings which we can divine by analysis are given to them and other concepts which are also used quite freely in the documentation – sometimes, as we have just seen, in the same sentence.

Many other terms are similarly used, of a kind which any student teacher knows are highly problematic in their meaning, and yet nowhere is this problematic aspect of these concepts acknowledged or any attempt made to offer clear definitions or interpretations of how they are to be understood. These are far too numerous to be explored individually here in detail. Terms such as 'potential', 'progression', 'continuity', 'coherence', 'skills', 'processes', 'understanding', 'achievement', 'abilities', 'development', 'experience' and many more litter the 1988 Act and especially its supporting documentation; they are never defined or explained or even discussed; and yet all are highly controversial; all have been, and continue to be, the subjects of long and inconclusive debate and of recognized definitional uncertainty; and all demand, and are entitled to, continued exploration and discussion.

We must note the lack of such discussion, and indeed awareness of the need for it, in the planning of the National Curriculum, and we must also, therefore, record the intellectual impoverishment which characterizes that planning. More specifically, however, we must note four things.

First, it is the case that the absence of any stated definition of terms and concepts which are capable of many definitions means that, in order to evaluate the conceptual structure of the National Curriculum, we must, as we have just seen in relation to the concepts of 'standards' and 'balance and breadth', divine the meanings to be placed on these terms from an examination of other aspects both of the regulations for and the practical implementation of that curriculum. We have to look at the context in which they are used to provide us with clues as to the definitions or interpretations which must be placed on them in that context.

Second, we must note that that content makes it quite clear that all these concepts are viewed in relation to the subjects and the subject content of the National Curriculum and not by reference to the development of the individual pupil's learning. 'Progression', 'continuity', 'coherence', 'development' and all the other terms we see are used to describe the pupil's passage through the successive stages of each subject, as defined in the attainment targets and programmes of study, and contain no reference to, or implications for, the individual pupil's response to what is offered. They are applied to the objects of learning rather than to the subjects who are engaged in the learning process, to the 'official' rather than to the 'received' curriculum, to teaching rather than to learning, and it is that perspective or reference point which is the clue to their conceptual significance and to their meaning. This may well represent a major fallacy, a 'category error'. It is certainly fallacious and misleading to endow them, in the search for an acceptable rhetoric, with overtones of a quite different set of meanings, those derived from notions of individual development. And the meaning which on analysis they are seen clearly to bear in this context reflects again the thinking, philosophy and ideology of the National Curriculum.

Third, we must note that, since we have no detailed definitions of these individual concepts, we must rely not only on the context but also on the total picture to provide us with an understanding of that underlying rationale which we attempted to identify in our last section. It is this, in the event, which gives support and justification to the claims which were made there in relation to the basic philosophy of the National Curriculum. If, through lack of definition, individual terms have the force only of rhetoric, then judgement and evaluation must be of the whole.

Fourth, we must note that this lack of definition leads also to the kinds of conceptual incompatibility and incoherence we have described. If terms are not defined it becomes easy to muddle them. When clear definitions are divined by analysis of the contexts in which they are used, then, almost inevitably, some of those definitions are seen to be incompatible with others and the whole conceptual framework is revealed as lacking coherence. In terms of intellectual quality, the National Curriculum is a mile wide but only an inch deep.

We must finally note that the failure or unwillingness to recognize the problematic nature of these concepts and the use of them as though they can bear only one fixed meaning must have the effect of ossifying those concepts within those meanings, or, to put it differently, of stifling what should in relation to each of them be a continuing debate. If our understanding of the complexities of educational planning and practice is to continue to grow and develop, there must be continuing debate of their conceptual infrastructure. Failure to acknowledge that is to risk arresting all such development.

This takes us naturally on to a further issue we must explore in our conceptual evaluation of the National Curriculum. That is, the extent to which it reveals an awareness of, an appreciation of and a response to the many conceptual understandings of curriculum and of curriculum planning which we have already acquired through detailed work in this field in recent years. It is not enough to base our evaluative judgements on an assessment of the internal clarity and coherence of these policies; we must also consider the quality of the understanding they display of the field in which they purport to be operating.

CONCEPTUAL ISSUES IN CURRICULUM PLANNING

There are several important respects in which our understanding of the complexities of curriculum planning and development has been extended in recent years. It has become apparent, for example, both from the experience of those who have been engaged in curriculum innovation and from reflection upon their experience, that one can adopt several quite distinct approaches towards curriculum planning, and that, as a result of this kind of insight, due attention must be paid by any curriculum planner to the selection of the approach appropriate to his or her purposes. Second, in parallel with this, we have acquired, as we saw earlier, a much clearer view of the subtleties of the process of evaluation and, especially, the need for it to be planned in phase and in harmony with the planning model we have chosen to adopt.

It will be apparent, therefore, that any exercise in curriculum planning, from that of the individual teacher to that of the national planner, must take account of these understandings and certainly must be evaluated against the perspectives they offer. Strictly, such planning should include explanations of how it has taken such account and/or why it has chosen its particular model or approach, so that its thinking can be evaluated in the light of such explanations. If, however, its choice is not clarified or explained, evaluation again must begin by divining from an examination of the actualities of the curriculum which has been planned what choices have been made, and, if possible, why, so that again these can be assessed in terms of their appropriateness and their coherence as well as in terms of whether we approve them or not.

We must now explore both these sources of understanding in slightly more detail, in order to be able to use them both as a route to a fuller understanding of the conceptual base of the National Curriculum and, again, as a measure of its quality.

Models of curriculum planning

Many words have been expended on the debate over models of curriculum planning in recent years, beginning with assertions which were being made quite early in the present century. It is a long-running debate. And it is this, more than anything else, which makes the absence of any reference to that debate throughout all the explanatory material which has been published in connection with the National Curriculum most surprising. The ramifications of this debate are many and there is not space here to explore them all in detail. A summary must, therefore, suffice.

Broadly speaking, the development of this debate has been as follows. It began to be felt, first, that curriculum planning lacked precision and structure (as compared, for example, with the techniques which had been developed for the planning of industrial processes) and, second, that too much educational planning was taking a form little more sophisticated than statements of the knowledge to be transmitted by the teacher and assimilated or learnt by the pupil. In short, it was claimed that there was little or no real planning of the curriculum and that teachers were merely taking the subjects and the subject content which had, largely by tradition, grown to be the main areas of teaching in schools and teaching them in a largely unplanned, even haphazard, way. The planning of each lesson or series of lessons might be done with great care but there was a lack of any real overall scheme, except such as might be provided by syllabuses, especially those of the examination boards.

This concern led to two main, and related, types of proposal. The first of these was that we should break down the subject content of our teaching into a progression of small 'bites' or steps, in order to give ourselves and our pupils a clearly structured *course* of learning – what has been called the 'Thirty-Nine Steps' approach to teaching. The assumption of this was that all learning must be seen as a linear process, as a matter of progression from easy to more difficult stages, and that this linear process can and must be set out as the only satisfactory form of clear and concise curriculum planning.

The second, rather different but nevertheless related, proposal was that we should first set out the *aims* of our curriculum, and then translate those aims into another kind of 'Thirty-Nine Steps' progression of 'objectives'. Again, therefore, the proposal is that we adopt for our planning a linear structure, but the elements in that structure are now short- and medium-term objectives which will lead us inexorably towards ultimate aims, rather than small and simple chunks of knowledge content leading to larger and more difficult pieces, and, finally, presumably to some kind of subject mastery.

It will be clear how these two approaches or models are related. Primarily, this is because they both view education as a linear process. It will also be apparent, however, that they differ in several significant ways. Perhaps the most important of these is their different starting points. For the first begins from statements of the content to be transmitted and plans its stages by reference to that; while the second begins with statements of long-term aims, plans its steps as stages in the progression toward the attainment of those aims and, most important, regards the selection of the content of the curriculum as a device for achieving those objectives and those aims and not as its prime concern.

We thus have what is often called a 'content' model of curriculum planning and an 'aims and objectives' model. It can be seen too that they can sometimes be conflated, since, if our long-term aim is the mastery of a certain body or bodies of subject knowledge, then the step-by-step planning is of objectives which will be framed in terms of content. Thus we often find statements of curricular plans or projects which contain both outlines of content and lists of objectives. This can be done coherently, however, only when the mastery of subjects is the prime concern, the aim of the process. (And even in such cases it may be asked whether, once the content has been specified, any statement of objectives is necessary.) It will be plain, therefore, that it does not make sense to offer statements of long-term aims expressed in non-subject terms (such as the development of the individual), accompanied by statements of short-term objectives which are expressed as subject content.

This, then, offers us one criterion for evaluating the National Curriculum. For the 1988 Act itself and its supporting documentation speak both of subjects and of 'aims and objectives'. These 'aims and objectives', as we have seen, are in many places expressed in terms of the development of pupils, or indeed, of society: 'the spiritual, moral, cultural, mental and physical development of pupils . . . and of society' (1988 Act, s.1(2)). Yet the curriculum is then broken down, as we have also seen, first, into a list of core and foundation subjects and, second, within each subject into a series of attainment targets, clearly 'based on the objectives model of education' (Nuttall, 1989, p. 53) and defined in terms of the content of that subject. We thus have, it would seem, exactly that kind of conflation of the two models which cannot make logical sense or coherence. Either the aims *are* the subjects, and the mastery of these subjects, or the subjects are subservient to the aims. To put it simply, it cannot be assumed that the aim of promoting the spiritual, moral, cultural, mental and physical development of pupils will be attained by exposing all to exactly the same subjects and taking them all through those subjects by exactly the same step-by-step route as set out in the attainment targets. If it were attained, it could only be by accident; and that is the very antithesis of planning.

It is a highly simplistic approach to curriculum planning to begin from a list of the subjects the curriculum is to contain, with no indication even of why these subjects have been selected. There are no intrinsic merits in any subjects as such. What is important about subjects in the curriculum is the educational aims they are intended to achieve. Subjects must be 'treated as means not as ends. Virtually all the enlightened views on curriculum planning are now agreed that subjects should be regarded as important only if they help to reach other objectives which, in turn, have to be justified' (Lawton, 1987). The crucial forms of justification for any subjects themselves in the curriculum, therefore, are explications of *how* they are expected to achieve these aims and 'why these subjects have been chosen in preference to other ways by which aims might be realized' (White, 1988, p. 115). And those other ways raise questions about the potential of approaches to curriculum planning other than via lists of subjects. In short, it is a manifestly unsophisticated form of curriculum which, in the 1980s, merely lists the subjects of which it will consist, declares the overall aims which it purports to have and hopes, or assumes, that there is, or will be, some connection between the two. Conceptually this is not the case; empirically it is unlikely to be the case; and a properly constructed curriculum would not be based on such slender hopes and assumptions, let alone on such a muddled set of conceptions. 'The curriculum . . . has to be presented as more than a series of subjects and lessons in the timetable' (DES, 1980, p. 3).

Further, there is nothing sacrosanct about school subjects. For it has been shown with total conviction (Goodson, 1983) that subjects do not enjoy some kind of God-given status but are to be seen very clearly as human creations. As such, they themselves change and develop, or are changed and developed, and that process must be allowed to continue. To create a curriculum which merely lists its core and foundation subjects and their content is not only to ignore this but also to create a context in which those subjects are likely to become ossified in their fixed form and conception. We will see later that it is a form of curriculum which inhibits all curriculum development; we must note here that it acts as a bar against the development of its constituent subjects too.

Over the years a number of other criticisms have been made of both these models, whether taken singly or together. These criticisms, therefore, must relate also to the planning model adopted for the National Curriculum and go beyond questions of its internal coherence. It has been pointed out, for example, that the 'aims and objectives' model by definition reflects an instrumental view of education, and we noted in Chapter 2 what many people have found unsatisfactory in that. We should note, then, that the adoption of that model for the National Curriculum, albeit in a confused form, and whether it is consistently adhered to or not, is further evidence for the claim made earlier that it is itself essentially instrumental.

Second, in criticism of both these models, it has been claimed that learning, and especially that form of learning which is to be regarded as part of an *educational* process, is never the linear, step-by-step progression both the models assume and advocate. It is difficult to think of any learning, even that of the most basic of 'skills', which can be accurately characterized in this way. And if this is true of the most simplistic forms of learning, it must manifestly be true of those more sophisticated forms of learning which constitute educational development. Learning is a far more subtle process than that, and one where we come at things from many different angles and perspectives and sometimes have to do so over and over again before we attain real understanding. It has been likened to a spiral staircase rather than a rope-ladder. It is a matter of holistic capability, and that can never be a mere aggregation of parts.

This, then, has been another criticism of the 'Thirty-Nine Steps' views of educational planning. A concern with content need not of course necessarily lead to the adoption of this model. But when it does, as in the National Curriculum's conceptualization of subjects in terms of a progression of ten incremental levels within attainment targets, it is vulnerable to this kind of criticism. The 'aims and objectives' model, on the other hand, must of necessity lead to this kind of linearity. This is why we hinted in Chapter 1 that we cannot accept too readily or uncritically the claim of the TGAT Report (DES, 1988a, para. 2) that 'a school can function effectively only if it has adopted . . . clear aims and objectives'.

Those who have criticized both these models, on the grounds we have noted and many others, have urged upon us a third, quite different approach. They have suggested, first, that a more appropriate, satisfactory and, indeed, workable basis for curriculum planning – again at any level, including that of the individual teacher – is the prespecification not of content or of 'aims and objectives' but of procedural principles, that aims should be translated not into a hierarchical sequence of short-term objectives but into a statement of the principles which are to inform the implementation of the curriculum at every stage and level (Stenhouse, 1975). This approach, they claim, enables the aims or the essence of the curriculum plan to be kept constantly to the fore, so that it establishes a clear structure for practice, but at the same time it makes possible the kind of flexibility of interpretation and adaptation to particular pupils and contexts which every teacher knows are of the essence not only of education but also of any productive form of learning.

In short, this model recognizes the central role the teacher must play in any *educational* process. Education cannot be conducted by 'remote control' or by central management. Outside agencies can only set guidelines or parameters within which teachers must be free to act and to make their professional judgements. Any attempt to impose restrictions which go beyond that and offer detailed, step-by-step, blueprints for teaching must seriously diminish the quality of educational provision.

This 'process' model, as it has come to be called, has been further refined by some into what is now known as a 'developmental' model (Blenkin and Kelly, 1987, 1988). For it has been argued that it is a model which lends itself, in a way that the others cannot, to a view of and an approach to education as the development of each individual child's potential and capacities, the basic procedural principles of this process being set out in developmental terms and thus providing the criteria by which judgements can constantly be made about the development of each child and the provision which must be made to support that development. It has also been argued for some time, and with some force, that this model of curriculum and this approach to education are so fundamentally different from the others as to be quite incompatible with them. It is for this reason, among many others, that the National Curriculum is likely to have a particularly distorting effect on the curriculum of the primary school, and especially on early childhood education, where a 'developmental' philosophy has long held sway (Blenkin and Kelly, 1987, 1988).

Two further points, therefore, can now be made in our critical evaluation of the National Curriculum. We claimed earlier that the notion of education as personal development is not what the National Curriculum is concerned with. We can now see why that claim was made and part of the justification for it. For, if the proponents of the developmental model are right to assert its incompatibility with other approaches, then it is inaccurate, even improper, for the architects of the National Curriculum to claim that it is designed to meet both the economic needs of society and at the same time the developmental needs of the individual, that it is intended to promote 'the . . . development of pupils . . . and of society' (1988 Act, s. 1(2)). If it succeeds in doing so in some cases, then we have to say again that that will be purely a matter of accident, and thus, as we said earlier, the very antithesis of planning. It might be argued, therefore, that those who have planned the National Curriculum are themselves in breach of the 1988 Act, since the curriculum they have planned will not meet the requirements the Act itself makes of them.

Second, the very existence of this model of planning, irrespective of its particular form or nature, makes it incumbent on all planners, as we said earlier, to make a deliberate choice and to give reasons for that choice. If this approach is rejected, as it clearly has been in the planning of the National Curriculum, there really is an obligation on its planners to say, if not why they have rejected it, then at the very least why they have chosen the alternatives. One can, therefore, offer the further criticism that the choice of planning models has not been explained, so that perhaps that choice has been made in ignorance rather than after any degree of deliberation. This would explain, at least in part, that lack of coherence in the model which has been adopted which we noted earlier. Whatever the case, whether it is a matter of unexplained choice or of ignorance of the alternatives, there is a strong and valid criticism to be made.

Finally, it is worth noting that again, because we have not been offered this kind of explanation, we have to seek to divine what model has been adopted or, since the planning has clearly not been as precise or as professional as that, what model is implicit in the practices which have been advocated and followed in the implementation of the National Curriculum. The words in which it has been stated and explained carry with them many contradictions, as we have already noted, so that we must go beyond the rhetoric to the reality. That reality is an underlying rationale of the kind we identified earlier – instrumental, focused on the economic needs of society and consequently élitist – overlaid by a muddled and incoherent conceptual structure, a conceptual structure which will not bear close analysis, and which, as a result, provides not a sound theoretical base for this new educational programme but a mass of rhetoric, whose effect, if not its intention, is to conceal the stark realities.

Again, therefore, we must note the intellectual impoverishment of these new policies.

Evaluation theory

The second, and related, area of theoretical understanding which we suggested we should be able to look for evidence of in a national curriculum designed in the 1980s is that of evaluation theory. We need not perhaps devote as much space to this as we have to our discussion of curriculum models, since we made several major points about it at the beginning of this chapter in relation to our own attempts at an evaluation of the National Curriculum itself. We noted, for example, an important distinction between summative and formative evaluation; and we also identified that all-important distinction between empirical and conceptual evaluation, and especially between evaluation of the effects of a curricular programme and of its worth or value.

We must, however, pick up both these points here in relation to what we have subsequently said about curriculum models. For, first, we should note that, while summative forms of evaluation are perfectly appropriate to 'aims and objectives' and to content-based approaches to education and curriculum, they have no place in the evaluation of a process or developmental curriculum, to which no notion of summation can be assigned. Development is an ongoing and never completed process, so that logically it cannot be evaluated summatively. Claims, then, that the National Curriculum is concerned with development must be matched by an acceptance of the need for formative evaluation. There is no evidence that it is. It is in fact quite clear that no such facility exists. Formative evaluation implies the possibility of modification and change; and that is not a possibility that exists in any real sense within a curriculum which is as rigidly controlled from the centre as we have seen the National Curriculum to be. Again, then, we divine that it is not a developmental curriculum in any sense, whatever the rhetoric, and that it is, as we have claimed, instrumental, concerned with outcomes, and thus is appropriately to be evaluated by summative means.

Second, we must note that there is no obvious intention to evaluate its worth as an educational curriculum. It is possible, as we have seen, that modifications may be made to profile components or levels or attainment targets within the approved subjects in the light of experience. There is little evidence, however, of any intention that these modifications should go beyond adjustments in the light of the response of pupils to them or that research is to be undertaken or attention given to assessing the value of this particular range of subjects or of the conceptions of those subjects with which the working groups have presented us. Indeed, the whole paraphernalia for the development of standard assessment tasks (SATs) at all of the key stages is such as to create a structure far too rigid to cope with any but the most minor of modifications. It is taking about three years to develop SATs to assess performance in relation to the attainment targets already identified and fixed. It is also costing a great deal of money, not to mention time and energy. It is thus inconceivable that the attainment targets will be changed or modified, and thus a need created to generate a whole new range of SATs to match these modifications. Thus, any evaluation of the worth of this curriculum will create problems of an almost completely intractable kind, and will be an embarrassment to all concerned. For, while such evaluation may point up the need for change, the rigid structure of the system as a whole militates against any change of substance being implemented or even contemplated. We cannot afford several million pounds to develop new SATs each year to meet changes in the attainment targets. This constitutes, too, another reason why the evaluation of the National Curriculum cannot be formative in any real sense, since the notion of formative evaluation entails a facility for change, adaptation and development. Furthermore, we might note finally that the separation of the functions, on the one hand, of defining and implementing the National Curriculum from, on the other, assessing it, through the creation of the two separate bodies, NCC and SEAC, creates both a further divide and a further barrier to any kind of change or development, at least of a substantive kind, and perhaps offers further evidence of an unwillingness to encourage such development by marrying the two.

This takes us on to a further and final point. Developments in evaluation theory have also revealed that the assessment of pupil performance has only a limited contribution to make to evaluation of the curriculum, and certainly that it must not be equated with curriculum evaluation. Again, however, it does appear that the force of this is not fully appreciated in the new policies. For the only kind of evaluation one hears of, and the only work that SEAC has as yet undertaken, has been in relation to the assessment of pupils at the several key stages.

One of the reasons for this is that a prime purpose, perhaps *the* prime purpose, of assessment in the National Curriculum is teacher appraisal and accountability. It is clear that the main source of data for teacher appraisal and the main criteria for teacher accountability will be the test scores of their pupils, since these will be deemed to reflect the efficiency of their 'delivery' of the programmes of study. We thus have a 'bureaucratic' rather than a 'professional' model of account- ability (Sockett, 1976; Elliott, 1976), what Lawrence Stenhouse (1975, p. 185) described as the 'systematic efficiency model'. This is a crude model whose major focus is on the economic issues of resource allocation and value for money, and which views the teacher as accountable to those who allocate the resources, i.e. the government, rather than to parents or pupils, and especially not to their professional peers. It is a model which assumes that education is con- cerned to bring about only a limited range of outcomes (Elliott, 1976), 'that achievement scores can be used to assess the causal effectiveness of what teach- ers do in classrooms' (op. cit., p. 49) and that teachers have little or no right to participation in the accountability process. The teacher is viewed as the techni- cian who 'delivers' the curriculum and whose performance can and must be judged solely on the efficiency of that 'delivery'.

There are many inadequacies in such a model, which can be summed up by asserting its general tendency to 'destroy schools as places where *education* goes on' (op. cit., p. 51). And it is for this reason that the alternative 'professional' or 'democratic' model has been advocated, a model which has underpinned many recent developments in school self-evaluation and peer evaluation, and has led to an awareness that a proper form of curriculum evaluation has to go beyond 'measurement' and embrace some attempt at qualitative and judgemental assessment. What is important to note here, however, is that it is this concern with a narrow form of bureaucratic accountability which limits the concept and the scope of curriculum evaluation within the National Curriculum and restricts the data to be used in its evaluation to that derived from pupil assessments. Together these would seem likely to ensure that evaluation will not go beyond some kind of measurement of the effectiveness of teachers, collectively and individually, in 'delivering' the National Curriculum, and that the assumption will continue to be made that the National Curriculum itself has sprung, perfect and fully formed, from the head of Mr Baker, like the goddess Athene from the head of Zeus.

It should not surprise us to find that we have a somewhat simplistic view of evaluation as well as that rather simplistic view of curriculum we noted earlier. One should not look to politicians to display levels of professional sophistication in fields where they have no professional understanding, or perhaps where they have vested interests. One remembers the comments of Denis Lawton (1977, p. 161), made a dozen years ago, that 'educational theory is much more difficult to indulge in than is generally realized by Labour politicians' and that 'Conservative politicians are in this respect luckier – they have no need of a theory to preserve the status quo or move backwards a little'. One remembers that, when in 1974 the Assessment of Performance Unit (APU) was set up, as its name suggests, to assess pupil performance, the expectations held of it at the outset, certainly by the politicians, were that it would do just that and no more. Its subsequent work, however, has itself contributed to the development of evaluation theory into something more sophisticated than that. And this would seem to constitute clear evidence that, when professional educators confront the realities of educational evaluation, they immediately recognize the inadequacies of simplistic forms. The work of the APU has now been subsumed under that of SEAC, and it does appear that the more subtle aspects of that work are being lost, largely owing to the new emphasis, or re-emphasis, on pupil assessment as the central focus and the main source of data for curriculum evaluation, and the use of that data for accountability rather than for educational purposes.

Again, therefore, we note that the implications of this are for summative rather than formative evaluation, for empirical evaluation, perhaps narrowed to encompass little more than the efficiency of 'delivery', rather than any conceptual evaluation of what is to be, or is being, 'delivered'. We note again, too, that nowhere is this made explicit, nowhere are we offered a theoretical explanation or justification of the approach to evaluation which is being adopted; that again we have, as a result, to divine what the theoretical and conceptual base of evaluation policy is; and finally, that, when we seek to discover this through an examination of the actual practices and the implementation of these policies, we see once more evidence that supports those claims we made in the first part of this chapter that the underlying rationale of the National Curriculum is instrumental, commercial and, as a result, élitist. To that we can now add that the structure created to ensure its efficient 'delivery' is rigid and inflexible, allowing no scope for a developmental or process approach to curriculum or for a formative scheme of evaluation. Further, there is no mechanism for adaptation or change, only a massive piece of machinery to maintain and drive what has already been determined and fixed. It is a steamroller rather than a Rolls-Royce; and it has the same instrumental functions and features.

SUMMARY AND CONCLUSIONS

This chapter has attempted to make a conceptual evaluation of the National Curriculum, to assess its underlying rationale or philosophy. We noted that the 1988 Act itself and its supporting documentation offer no clear statement of this underlying rationale. Our only course, therefore, has been to attempt to divine what it is, to work out for ourselves what its philosophy is, by analysis of the principles which seem to inform its provisions and the steps taken to implement it.

In attempting this analysis, we came to the conclusions, first, that its documentation lacks both conceptual clarity and conceptual coherence, that it appears to offer a rhetoric which is both at odds with the reality and inconsistent within itself; and, second, that the reality masked by that rhetoric is a curriculum which is fundamentally instrumental, commercial and élitist, and, consequently, of a form which inhibits any approach to education which might attempt to offer provision framed in terms of what might be the requirements of pupils as individuals. We noted that these assertions are likely to be challenged by the architects of the National Curriculum, but suggested that such a challenge could be based only on their rhetoric and that the exploration we have undertaken of the realities, of the actual conceptual structure of the scheme, served to confirm the assertions we had made about its basic philosophy and rationale.

Finally, we considered some recent developments in our theoretical understanding of curriculum design, and indicated that these offer a more sophisticated base for curriculum planning; that they offer greater scope for conceptual clarity in such planning; that they widen the range of choice open to curriculum planners; and that they thus oblige those who would make curriculum plans at any stage or level to give reasons for their choices and to provide a clear and coherent conceptual structure for their plans. This we saw the planners of the National Curriculum have failed to do, so that this failure in itself must constitute a major part of our critique.

In general, the chapter has attempted to demonstrate that the conceptual structure of the National Curriculum is seriously flawed – it lacks clarity, it lacks coherence and it lacks all awareness of the subtleties of curriculum theory, and perhaps especially of evaluation theory. Further, it has attempted to reveal what the conceptual structure of the National Curriculum actually is, what its underlying rationale, philosophy, ideology are, so that a judgement may be made of its value, its worth and its desirability.

We said at the beginning of this chapter that this kind of conceptual evaluation is only one kind of evaluation which can be undertaken in advance of the National Curriculum becoming fully operative. For, having asked how far the architects of that curriculum have taken account of recent developments in our theoretical understanding of curriculum, we must also ask how far they have taken into consideration empirical studies, research which has revealed not merely the complexities and subtleties required of us in thinking about and planning curricula at the theoretical level, but, further, understandings of the actualities of teaching and learning, of pupils' reactions to what is presented to them, of the role of the teacher in the educational process, of the impact of different forms of assessment and many more such matters. It is to an exploration of how far the National Curriculum has taken into account research evidence of this kind that we turn in the next chapters.

4

THE NATIONAL CURRICULUM – AN
EMPIRICAL EVALUATION I: THE
ASSESSMENT AND TESTING PROGRAMME

Chapter 3 examined the conceptual underpinning of the National Curriculum and revealed not merely that that underpinning is, in too many places, vague, incoherent and even illogical, but also that a major reason for this is that the curriculum has been planned without reference to, and thus without benefit of, the many understandings which recent analytical studies of curriculum design, planning and development have made available to those wishing to engage in any of these activities in a properly informed manner.

This chapter and the next will explore the extent to which the architects of the National Curriculum have, or have not, similarly ignored the findings of empirical research in education and experience of educational practice. A great deal of such research has been undertaken in the past, as we shall see, and much valuable knowledge and understanding are consequently available to us to assist with sound curriculum planning. This chapter will endeavour to establish to what extent such knowledge and understanding have been drawn upon in the planning of the National Curriculum.

We must begin by noting that no research has been specifically undertaken in support of, or as a preliminary to, its implementation. One can think of no other field of human endeavour where it would be regarded as intellectually, or even morally, acceptable to institute such major changes of policy and practice without attempting first to obtain some supporting research data. The only justification for such action would be that adequate use had been made of data already available. Whether this is the case or not is the question that these chapters will address.

The initial signs, however, are not promising. Someone assured the House of Lords in the debate on the Education Bill that Baker had not invented the National Curriculum in his bath. Clearly, the person whose question elicited that assurance must have gained from somewhere the impression that he had. And one cannot but have sympathy with that person's suspicions and concerns. One forms the impression, for example, that those attainment targets which are the very bones of the National Curriculum are being to a large extent 'plucked from the air' by the members of the working groups, and that they represent more what they guess or feel children ought to have learnt at the end of each of the key stages than any knowledge or understanding on their part of what children might be capable of learning by those ages. They do seem to be what I have heard described as 'acts of faith' rather than informed judgements, and, while there are, as Kierkegaard once pointed out, areas of human endeavour or interest where nothing else but such 'acts of faith' or 'leaps in the dark' are possible for us, these are by definition areas where informed understanding and knowledge are neither available nor conceivable. To take such leaps through ignorance of, or, perhaps worse, a deliberate refusal to acknowledge, such understanding and knowledge is indefensible intellectually, and perhaps morally too.

Yet one can find no evidence that any of the groups working on the detailed planning and implementation of the National Curriculum has evinced any interest in research findings other than those which seemed to support and justify conclusions they had already reached or the policies they have been required to carry out. And, further, one picks up ominous suggestions that contrary evidence is not only ignored, or rejected, but in some cases even suppressed to avoid embarrassment – and, indeed, to discourage open debate.

Perhaps the best evidence of this is to be found in publications emerging from the DES and especially those from Her Majesty's Inspectorate (HMI). For, until about a decade ago, HMI publications were stimulating, challenging and valuable contributions to a continuing debate; they reflected the traditional role of the HMI of disseminating ideas and good professional practice and acting as watchdogs for quality within the teaching profession. The style, the tenor and, indeed, the quality of documents emanating from this source have changed remarkably during the last decade, as nothing has emerged which in any sense could be seen as a challenge to, or even a criticism of, official policies, and many of the lines of thinking which earlier publications had promoted have disappeared entirely from view – without comment or explanation. Indeed, all such documents now consist of nothing more than arguments, often, as we saw in Chapter 3, leaving much to be desired in terms of clarity and coherence, in support of official policies. Once it was possible to distinguish HMI publications from those emanating from the civil servants of the DES – in stance, in attitude and in levels of professional understanding. Sadly, such a distinction can no longer be made. Nothing which might stimulate critical evaluation of current policies gets through the net. Nothing can be published through official channels which does not have the approval of the Secretary of State. The appointment as HMI of non-teachers, of people whose background and experience are in industrial and commercial management, also reinforces and illustrates this change of role from educational and advisory to executive and managerial, and further reduces the possibility of professional advice and comment from this source. Her Majesty's inspectors have been promoted (or demoted) to chief superintendents.

Thus the general sense one gets is that the National Curriculum reflects, at the very least, a failure to take full account of what research has told us about many aspects of educational practice. This further suggests that there may be issues to be addressed not merely of its own intellectual quality as a piece of planning but also of its potential side-effects and its practicability. For some of the evidence available to us offers clear indications of the effects which seem to follow from some of the kinds of practice the National Curriculum requires, so that we can from that gauge some of the side-effects to be expected. Furthermore, in educational planning, as much as in any other sphere, it is necessary to know what can be done as well as to assert what ought to be done, to take account of what is possible as well as of what is regarded as desirable. The mere passing of an Act will not bring things about if those things are impracticable, and it will not be reasonable (although it is unlikely that that will prevent it happening) to hold teachers responsible for the 'non-delivery' of the National Curriculum if that curriculum has features which on known evidence make it impossible to 'deliver'. We might further note again that the kinds of conceptual confusion and incoherence we noted in Chapter 3 are also likely to make the implementation of certain aspects of the National Curriculum impossible, since, as we saw there, some of them are incompatible with one another.

There are three reasons, then, why a full critique of the National Curriculum requires that we attempt to assess the extent to which its planning has taken account of all the research evidence which has a bearing on its implementation. First, we must evaluate its own internal intellectual quality; second, we must consider some of the likely effects of aspects of it which reveal a lack of attention to evidence which is available; and, third, we must attempt to evaluate the practicalities of its implementation. These three aspects of this kind of empirical evaluation must be borne in mind throughout what follows.

There are several major areas of research evidence which have a direct bearing on the implementation of the National Curriculum in one or all three of these ways. First, there is the whole area of pupil assessment, a central element of the new policies. This will be the focus of the present chapter. Second, there is the mass of knowledge and understanding we now have in relation to how pupils learn, what motivates them, how they react to certain kinds of teaching approaches and to certain forms of curriculum, what they assimilate via the 'hidden' curriculum, and so on. Third, there has been considerable development in our understanding of the education of pupils with special educational needs as a result of attempts to implement the proposals of the Warnock Report (DES, 1978a). Fourth, there have been many studies of the role of the teacher in the educational process, and we must consider the implications of these for the changed role that teachers are required to adopt within the new context, as well as the impact of these changes on the teachers themselves. Finally, there is the experience that has been gained from many attempts at curriculum change, and from studies arising from these, of the problems and difficulties of disseminating curriculum innovation or, to put it differently, of changing and controlling the curriculum from outside each individual school, and without the full involvement of teachers at every stage. These last four major issues we will explore in Chapter 5.

NATIONAL CURRICULUM ASSESSMENT

There is no doubt that the most salient and significant feature of the National Curriculum is its elaborate programme for testing all pupils in the core subject areas at the four key stages: 7+, 11+, 14+ and 16+. This programme of testing is at the heart, and is indeed the base, of the National Curriculum, and it is this that determines the kind of curriculum it is. Other nations have a national curriculum; none has as extensive or as intensive a programme of testing. There is little doubt, therefore, that the National Curriculum is an assessment-led curriculum; indeed, it is a classic example of such a curriculum. A recent DES bulletin on the Education Reform Act (DES, 1989d) begins by asserting that 'assessment should be the servant, not the master, of the curriculum'. With this assertion one cannot but agree. One has to recognize, however, that in the context of the National Curriculum assessment programme it is no more than an assertion, since that programme clearly is the controlling mechanism of the National Curriculum. As Denis Lawton (1989a, pp. 11–12) has said, 'it would be wrong to see the tests as a way of reinforcing the national curriculum; it would be more credible to see the national curriculum as a crude framework for the testing programme'. The clearest indication of the assessment-led nature of the National Curriculum is the fact that the first stage of its planning was the work of the Task Group on Assessment and Testing (TGAT), which set up, as we saw in Chapter 1, the framework for this testing programme, a framework (of profile components, attainment targets and levels) into which the working groups for individual subjects have subsequently had to fit their proposals for, and, indeed, their conceptions of, the subjects for which they have been given responsibility, since the framework makes no allowance for the possibility of different subjects requiring quite different approaches to assessment.

The choice of a 'graded test' system of assessment also reinforces this view of the prior place given to assessment in the current policies. For 'graded test schemes involve the development of graded objectives in particular subject areas, and are clearly beholden to arguments concerning the need to provide learners with more information on a regular basis, particularly those arguments deriving from criterion-referencing and mastery learning' (Torrance, 1989, p. 187). Such graded tests 'are clearly tailored to a mechanistic, if not static, view of learning' (ibid.). Graded test schemes of this kind can be contrasted with profiling or records of achievement which 'in principle at least, take a rather more dynamic stance' (ibid.). In such approaches objectives are open to negotiation with pupils and are 'in no sense restrictive of the pursuit of other outcomes' (ibid.). They thus provide a basis of support for curriculum development of various kinds rather than imposing a fixed and constraining structure on the curriculum. They also offer an alternative which TGAT and the planners of the National Curriculum might have chosen, an alternative which retains certain key ideas such as ' "criteria", "diagnosis" and "formative assessment" ' (op. cit., p. 189), but is significantly different in that 'the reference point is the learner and his or her interests and aspirations, not a centrally determined curriculum' (ibid.).

The development of such approaches is still in its infancy, but then 'a national system of graded assessment as proposed by TGAT is completely untried anywhere in the world . . . and one may be tempted to ask whether we would not be better building on what we have already got, or at least are beginning to develop' (ibid.). Clearly, it would be better to build on that, were it not for the fact that our political masters are seeking greater control of the school curriculum than such schemes would enable them to enjoy, and recognize the assessment system as offering the most effective mechanism for such control.

It might not be completely irrelevant to note further, before we begin to consider or to evaluate in detail these assessment arrangements, one or two points which may be of some general significance. The first of these is that a very great interest has been, and continues to be, expressed in the new assessment procedures by many, if not all, of the major publishing houses. Several have provided significant sums of money in support of groups preparing bids for contracts to develop the standard assessment tasks for various key stages. In some cases this money has been provided in advance of contracts being secured, as a pump-priming or seed-corn exercise in support of a bid for a contract designed to lead to a flood or a harvest of some magnitude.

Furthermore, at least one such publishing house has set up a conference for teachers and others within the education service, designed, it would seem, to explore how or how far (but not, I think, *whether*) assessment can be used to raise educational standards.

This activity on the part of publishers indicates that in their view there are rich pickings to be had from this assessment programme. And that must raise the question whether the public money they hope to pocket from this source is being spent as wisely as it might be in support of the education of the nation's children.

Perhaps more serious than that, however, is the attempt, reflected in the setting up of conferences on assessment, to move educational thinking down the road that will be most conducive to the securing of these rich pickings. It may well be that assessment can be used to raise standards. The forms of exploration of that question which we need, however, are those that may tell us *whether* this is the case. And such explorations are unlikely to be encouraged, or to be led to best effect, by anyone who has a financial interest in one particular answer to that question.

It is also perhaps worth noting at the outset of our discussion of the assessment programme that it has not been established with total conviction that the raising of standards is its prime intention, let alone whether this might be its effect. This is plainly the rhetoric of the case that has been offered in its support, but it is at least as credible that its main thrust, as was suggested in Chapter 3 and reiterated above, is towards strengthening central control of teachers and schools and establishing a, somewhat simplistic, database for accountability and appraisal.

It may be salutary to bear these points in mind as we look in detail at the assessment programme and attempt to gauge its likely impact on the curriculum.

FORMATIVE, DIAGNOSTIC AND SUMMATIVE ASSESSMENT

The impact of the assessment programme will of course depend to a large extent on how the task of assessing every pupil at the four key stages is tackled, and especially on the nature of the standard assessment tasks (SATs) developed to accomplish that task. The official view one is offered is that the nature of the impact the SATs have on the curriculum will depend on the SATs themselves and is thus the responsibility of the SAT development teams. It must be noted, however, that the framework those teams have been provided with offers only limited scope for the development of anything which might be educationally worthwhile.

The TGAT Report (DES, 1988a), as we saw in Chapter 1, made a positive recommendation and indeed clearly stressed that assessment, certainly at the first three of the key stages, should be formative and diagnostic, defining 'formative' as being concerned 'that the positive achievements of a pupil may be recognised and discussed and the appropriate next steps be planned' (op. cit., para. 23) and 'diagnostic' as a form of assessment 'through which learning difficulties may be scrutinised and classified so that appropriate remedial help and guidance can be provided' (ibid.). It also indicated that it did not see the boundary between these two purposes 'as being sharp or clear' (op. cit., para. 27) and went on to recommend 'that the basis of the national assessment system be essentially formative, but designed also to indicate where there is need for more detailed diagnostic assessment' (ibid.). It further recommended that at age sixteen, but *not* at the earlier stages, 'it should incorporate assessment with summative functions' (ibid.), 'summative' having been defined earlier (op. cit., para. 23) as 'for the recording of the overall achievement of a pupil in a systematic way'. The report also suggested that, in order to promote that formative/diagnostic function, and, indeed, make it possible, 'all assessment information about an individual be treated as confidential and thus confined to those who need to know in order to help that pupil' (op. cit., para. 28).

The distinction between the formative/diagnostic function of assessment and its summative role is crucial. Much, therefore, hinges on whether it can be, or is, maintained in practice. One notes, therefore, with some dismay that it is a distinction which seems to have disappeared in the subsequent steps taken towards implementation. For the DES document, *National Curriculum: From Policy To Practice* (DES, 1989c), tells us that 'the national assessment system will serve several purposes' (op. cit., para. 6.2). It will be formative (the diagnostic function has been subsumed within this), summative, evaluative, informative and 'helpful for professional development' (i.e. of teachers) (ibid.). The erosion of the subtle distinctions the TGAT Report stressed is plain and may be seen as another example of that lack of conceptual clarity we noted in Chapter 3. Furthermore, it is made quite explicit that the 'summative' function is to be present at all the key stages: 'The results of tests and other assessments should be used both *formatively* to help better teaching and to inform decisions about the next steps for a pupil, and *summatively* at age 7, 11, 14 and 16 to inform parents about their child's progress' (op. cit., para. 6.4).

Thus we no longer have any attempt to defer summative assessment until 16+, and that distinction between the formative/diagnostic and the summative functions of assessment, which we suggested earlier is crucial and which was seen to be so by the authors of the TGAT Report itself, has already disappeared.

One reason for this disappearance may well be the impossibility of maintaining such a distinction in practice. It is a distinction which can readily be adhered to by the individual teacher in the process of making judgements about individual pupils. Indeed, the making of formative/diagnostic assessments, which are very positively non-summative, is part and parcel of any teacher's normal day-to-day practice. 'How is Johnny responding to the work?', 'How can I best take him

on?', 'What difficulties is Sarah experiencing?', 'How can she be properly helped?' are questions most teachers ask themselves daily, hourly, even by the
minute; and there is no suggestion in them of any kind of summation. This kind
of purely formative/diagnostic exercise is not possible, however, in the context of
a criterion-referenced and national system of standardized measurements. For the
mere fact of its standardization makes this an exercise in summative assessment,
even if at the same time it is intended as one of formative diagnosis. And the fact
that it is taking place in the context of a clearly delineated sequence of attainment
targets reduces the formative/diagnostic function to one of methodology – 'How
can I help Johnny to score better on the SATs?' rather than 'What kinds of
educational experience will or may bring him on?' – and thus emphasizes the
summative aspects of the exercise, the summative measurement of where each
pupil stands here and now in the linear sequence of attainment targets. In this
kind of context every act of assessment is an act of measurement and must be
summative; whatever else it may succeed in being at the same time, it must
record 'the overall achievement of a pupil in a systematic way' (DES, 1988a,
para. 23).

In such a system of national standardized testing of a summative kind, there is
a need for the greatest possible accuracy. It is one thing to say that the tests
suggest that a pupil needs this, that or the other kind of support, help, curriculum
diet, methods of approach – especially at the level of the individual teacher who
can adjust these regularly and constantly if the diagnosis proves to be less than
perfect. It is quite another matter to measure performance against nationally
standardized criteria, and to reveal and publish the results of that measurement
(even if only specifically to parents and in aggregated form to the general public),
if there is any doubt about the accuracy of such test results. Nor must we forget
the major administrative decisions which may be made on the basis of these test
scores, not only in the case of individual pupils (in respect of such things as their
allocation to groups, classes or even schools – especially the selective city
technology colleges), but also in relation to institutions (in respect of their status,
their funding, even their continued existence), since, as we saw in Chapter 1,
there are many implications for institutional security in the commercially competitive context which the 1988 Act has created for them.

Thus accuracy becomes a major concern, and, consequently, evidence we
already have about the accuracy of testing procedures used in the past becomes
highly relevant. This is an issue we must return to below.

TESTING AT 7+

We know little or nothing about the impact of national testing on pupils at 7+. It
has not been done before on a national scale in this country or in any other. And

we might perhaps note in passing that it thus represents a massive and wide-scale form of experimentation on generations of the nation's seven-year-olds. We noted in our introduction the desirability of accepting something like the ethics of the medical profession in educational planning – a refusal to experiment on human beings on moral grounds and a parallel concern to pre-test all potential new developments and to take advantage of all research and experiential evidence already available. We must note that neither of these safeguards has been adopted here and that a new policy has been introduced with neither an attempt to obtain research evidence nor apparently any awareness that such might be sought, so that the implementation of the policy itself on a full scale becomes an act of experimentation.

We can thus only speculate on what the potential effects might be of national testing on seven-year-olds. We should note that the TGAT Report (DES, 1988a) recommended that they should be tested in such a way that they would not know that they were in fact being tested, that the tests should 'seem to the children to be part of ordinary school work, though conducted in a standardised way by the teacher' (op. cit., para. 149). It is already clear, however, that the SATs which are being developed will not and cannot be administered in this unobtrusive manner. And, indeed, this, like the proposal to avoid summative assessment at this stage and the other early stages, may be another example of the fundamental impracticability of some of the TGAT recommendations. At the very least, a summative assessment made at age seven and published – if only to their parents – must lead to a high level of awareness of what is happening, and of its significance, on the part of all but those children fortunate enough to have been blessed with laid-back parents. It might thus be not unreasonable to expect those stresses and strains which we all remember were associated with the 11+ testing of old, nor to expect them to be even more in evidence in seven-year-olds. Indeed, there is already some evidence of the stressful effects of the use of diagnostic tests in mathematics on pupils of this age (Denvir and Brown, 1987).

In this connection it is worth noting that some local authorities are already in process of resurrecting or extending the special arrangements within their psychological services designed to deal with the stress problems created by the 11+, in order to prepare also for the comparable problems they now expect to face at 7+. And a side-effect of this is obviously a reduction in the resources available for pupils with other kinds of special need, those whose problems have not been created directly by the education system itself.

We can speculate in more detail and perhaps with more precision, however, by reference to what we know about the effects of streaming at 7+, which was once the practice in most junior schools. There is also a mass of evidence about the effects of testing at 11+. And again it is not unreasonable to expect this evidence to be equally, and perhaps especially, applicable at 7+.

EVIDENCE FROM STREAMING AND SELECTION PROCEDURES

Much of what we know from both of these sources relates to the accuracy – or rather the inaccuracies – associated with them. Before considering this evidence, however, it will be worthwhile remembering, first, that the *raison d' être* of the 11+ selection tests, and, indeed, of the tests upon which streaming was based, was that they were intended to be diagnostic, designed to select pupils for the most suitable form of educational provision, and, second, that the inaccuracies of both were such that streaming was abandoned by most primary schools as the • evidence of its effects began to emerge, and selective secondary schooling was abolished by law in 1965 (even though it continued to be practised in some areas – clear evidence perhaps of the difficulty of changing educational practices from the centre).

There is not the space here to review all the many research studies which devoted themselves to the issue of 11+ testing, its levels of accuracy and its effects. Indeed, one thought that these had been confined to history and their lessons learned, but the reappearance of national testing within the National Curriculum must bring about their resurrection, since their findings have to be seen as highly relevant to the new testing programme, and they offer the only hard evidence and experience we have against which to evaluate that programme.

The main messages which came from those studies were, first, that the level of accuracy achieved showed a degree of error larger than 10 per cent, or, to put it differently, more than one pupil in every ten was wrongly assessed (and thus wrongly placed with regard to secondary educational provision); second, that there is an inevitable backlash on to the curriculum pupils are offered as teachers struggle to overcome the known inaccuracies by 'teaching to the tests', by offering pupils those somewhat simplistic forms of educational experience which show up in formal tests; third, that several major factors could be identified as contributing to the inaccuracies of these procedures, including socio-economic background, ethnic origin and gender; and, fourth, that 'failure' in these tests leads in most cases to a lowering of levels of performance rather than to any raising of standards (and 'success' to a corresponding increase). It is perhaps worth looking briefly at each of these factors in turn, since they would all seem to be highly relevant to the testing programme that is currently being introduced.

ACCURACY OF ASSESSMENT

The inaccuracies of the 11+ testing system are well documented, as are those of the devices used to stream pupils, especially in primary schools. A very high proportion of children were shown to have been wrongly placed, whether in a streamed class at 7+ or in a selective secondary school at 11+. All the evidence pointed to the need to correct these errors. It was estimated that between 10 and 30 per cent of pupils would need to be transferred between streams in the junior school (Daniels, 1961). And at secondary level, many authorities instituted a 13+ examination to put right the errors of the 11+. However, the studies also showed that the actual levels of transfer were considerably lower than these figures would lead one to expect: 5 or 6 per cent in one study of streaming (Daniels, 1961), 2.3 per cent in another (Douglas, 1964), and 1 per cent the national figure for transfers into grammar schools at 13+ (Jackson, 1964). The reason for this is that, inaccurate or not, the results of these tests led to decisions which had a degree of permanence, an 'inbuilt finality of judgement, so hard to overmaster' (Jackson, 1964, p. 124), which made subsequent adjustment or correction very difficult. Clearly, the same will be the case if similar decisions are made on the basis of the new national testing programme, especially at 7+ and 11+. And who can be confident or optimistic or brave enough to assert that such decisions will not be made?

For such inaccuracies are inevitable in any kind of attempt at educational assessment which attempts to *measure* attainment. The more sophisticated aspects of educational development are impossible to measure with any degree of accuracy, at least when one is attempting to do this on a comparative and national scale. It is not difficult for an experienced teacher to make a formative/diagnostic assessment of an individual pupil as a basis for decisions about that pupil's educational diet, and to do this with a high degree of accuracy, precision and success. For such assessment is largely qualitative in nature. It is also judgemental. In fact, everything of real educational significance is a matter of individual judgement and cannot be *measured* with exactitude and precision. Thus the difficulty comes when we try to measure educational attainment in a quantitative and summative manner in relation to agreed national standards and by some form of common testing procedure. Matthew Arnold made this point over a century ago in commenting on the replacement of inspection by examination under the Revised Code of 1862. Under inspection, 'the whole life and power of a class, the fitness of its composition, its handling by the teacher were well tested; the Inspector became well acquainted with them, and was enabled to make his remarks on them to the head teacher, and a powerful means of correcting, improving and stimulating them was thus given' (quoted in Curtis, 1948, p. 262). This is something, he goes on to say, 'which the new examination does not and by its nature cannot supply' (op. cit., p. 263). And that is largely because, as he also points out, 'the aim and object of the new system of examination is not to develop the higher intellectual life of an elementary school, but to spread and fortify, in its middle and lower portions, the instruction in reading, writing, and arithmetic, supposed to be suffering' (op. cit., pp. 262–3). *Plus ça change . . .*

Assessing achievement qualitatively, then, is a matter of judgement not of measurement, and to attempt to assess qualitative achievement in quantitative terms or by quantitative measures is to attempt to square the circle, and must deteriorate into a policy of 'never mind the quality, feel the width'. Educational quality cannot be measured, and canot even be properly assessed by quantitative tests, however sophisticated. One assumes that it was for this reason that the TGAT Report (DES, 1988a) recommended the additional use of teacher assessments in the testing programme. It suggested that there should be group moderation in which the results of the national assessments through the standard assessment tasks and assessments made by the pupils' own teachers might be reconciled. It further suggested, however, that, since this would be time consuming, it could not happen in all cases and that, when it did not happen, the 'test results should override the teacher assessment if there is any discrepancy' (Nuttall, 1988, p. 56). Subsequently, the Secretary of State has declared this system to be not only complicated but also costly, and has asked that a simpler and cheaper system be devised. There is little doubt that such a system will entail a reduction in the level and significance of teacher assessment, since it is that which is both costly and complicated.

It is also the case that this debate may now be of little more than academic interest, since Mrs Thatcher herself has overruled the advice of everyone on this matter, and decreed that pupils will be assessed only by the national tests, or at least that only the results of these are to be used for reporting to parents. She has suggested that teachers' judgements might be biased and untrustworthy (i.e. that teachers cannot be trusted to be professional); that the sophisticated proposals of the TGAT Report would be too complex and expensive to implement (i.e. that educational assessment can be and should be done on the cheap); and that the demands made on teachers' time should be kept to a minimum. We might note in passing the powers that the 1988 Act gives to the government to make decisions of this kind without further consultation. We might perhaps also note that this decision has been strongly criticized by the joint council for the GCSE in respect of its denial to teachers of the right to adjust individual test scores in the light of their knowledge of pupils' work. It accused the School Examinations and Assessment Council (SEAC) of undervaluing teachers' professional judgement and reducing the validity of the tests, which would inevitably, it claimed, have a lower level of reliability and would have unfortunate consequences for the children concerned.

Yet there is evidence to support the view that teachers' assessments of their pupils' work are as reliable as any form of examination or testing other than objective tests (Connaughton, 1969). The advantages of school-based examining are 'that the assessment may be made by an examiner (the teacher) who knows the pupils, who can assess them over a period of time, and can make use of different types of examination as often as he feels they need to be used' (op. cit., p. 174). The main difficulty is the problem of standardizing such assessments across schools. Even so, this is a difficulty which seems not to have made for greater problems of marker reliability than the standardization of the marking of essay-type examinations by different examiners. And it is one which seems to have been satisfactorily absorbed within the GCSE and in many schemes under the Technical Vocational and Educational Initiative.

However, it remains, and always will remain, true that complete accuracy of assessment will never be achieved by any of these means. The only device for achieving anything approaching total accuracy is the objective, multiple-choice test, since 'the more specific and detailed the examining procedures to be followed, the more reliable and valid the examinations tend to be' (Connaughton, 1969, p. 173).

The only way, then, in which we can hope to achieve any acceptable degree of accuracy in national testing is to adopt agreed national standards and criteria which are highly simplistic. If we cannot discover with total accuracy how many pupils in the country at age seven can multiply 3 by 4 and get 12, then there is something highly inefficient about our test instruments. Such total accuracy will be impossible to attain, however, if our concern is with how many pupils have reached what is seen as an appropriate level of numeracy or of mathematical understanding, since these are far less easy to define and impossible to *measure* on a national scale since they do not lend themselves to any form of *measurement*. This was one reason why the Assessment of Performance Unit was reluctant to attempt to monitor pupil progress in such areas as personal and social development and aesthetics. However, even in the areas it has monitored, whenever it has sought to get to grips with more sophisticated aspects of educational development, such as the ability to think scientifically, creative writing or design and technological capability, it has had to recognize that its test results must be less than 100 per cent accurate. And, while a lower level than that is acceptable within the context of a research study, designed not to assess individuals but to secure an overall picture of the state of the art in particular subject areas, that level of accuracy is clearly unacceptable when one is measuring the attainment of individual pupils, informing them and their parents of their levels of attainment and possibly making far-reaching decisions about the future educational provision for them.

IMPACT ON THE CURRICULUM

It is this that leads us on to our second main point, the backlash effects that such testing has on the curriculum. It is quite clear that the 11+ governed the curriculum of most primary schools at least in their fourth year and sometimes throughout the school. It is equally plain that the demands of public examinations at 16+, certainly in the days before the teachers themselves were involved in the examination, have determined the curriculum of secondary schools, usually in the two final years but again quite often, and in some subjects more than others, throughout the five-year period of secondary education. In fact, as long ago as 1864, the Clarendon Report noted that it is possibly an inevitable effect of examinations to be directive of the curriculum, to determine what it will contain or consist of, rather than testing what it has been decided for other reasons should be there. More recently, this was reiterated by the Beloe Report (SSEC, 1960). We may also note a further comment made by Matthew Arnold on the impact of the Revised Code of 1862:

> I cannot say that the impression made upon me by the English schools at this second return to them has been a hopeful one. I find in them, in general, if I compare them with their former selves, a deadness, a slackness, and a discouragement which are not the signs and accomplishments of progress. If I compare them with the schools of the Continent I find in them a lack of intelligent life much more striking now than it was when I returned from the Continent in 1859. This change is certainly to be attributed to the school legislation of 1862.
>
> (quoted in Curtis, 1948, p. 263)

He also claimed that 'examinations and payment by results deprived children of liberal education, and teachers of their rightful freedom' (Curtis and Boultwood, 1960, p. 142). Thus, it seems that, wherever there is a public examination or testing system, the curriculum must inevitably be assessment-led, with all the implications that has for the climate of the school as well.

Furthermore, if we are right in claiming – and the evidence certainly supports such a claim – that accuracy of assessment requires simplicity of educational goals, that the more simple the targets we set ourselves the greater degree of accuracy we will achieve in assessing the attainment of pupils, then one of the major effects of an assessment-led curriculum is likely to be that it will become simplified. The more sophisticated and subtle aspects of educational experience will escape our assessment nets, whose meshes will be far too large to catch them, and they will thus become devalued as teachers succumb to the temptation to 'teach to the tests', as they once did in preparation for the 11+ and as many of them continue to do at 16+.

In relation to primary schools, for example, it has been suggested, on the basis of a comparison of England and France, where primary schools are characterized by 'a dull, repetitive and harsh pedagogy' (Broadfoot and Osborn, 1987), that such teaching to the tests in English (and Welsh) primary schools is likely to lead to 'the sacrifice . . . of that warm and creative learning environment that has made English primary schools the envy of many parts of the world' (ibid.). And Caroline Gipps (1988, p. 71) has listed several 'generalizable characteristics that seem to be common to primary schools today' on which 'regular and significant examining . . . will . . . on the basis of what we know already about the effects of testing, have an impact'. These are:

- – mixed ability classes
- – little overt competition between children
- – a certain informality in the relationship between teacher and child
- – a variety of teaching and learning approaches
- – the integration of some subjects into topic work
- – few 'lessons' in formal subjects, other than maths.

(Gipps, 1981, p. 71)

That teachers narrow the focus of their teaching when faced with narrow forms of assessment is clear. That the need for accuracy will lead to such narrow forms of assessment is also clear. And, indeed, we are told officially that, when detailed results of assessment are given in full to parents, 'the Government attaches great importance to the principle that these reports should be simple and clear' (DES, 1989c, para. 6.4). Simplicity, then, is not merely the effect; it is also the goal. And simplicity of assessment implies a concentration on the more simple dimensions of teaching and learning, and in particular on products rather than processes. Elliot Eisner (1985, p. 7) has graphically warned us of the dangers of this kind of procedure: 'To fish for trout in a stream using bait designed for salmon, and to conclude from our failed efforts that no trout are there, is to draw what might very well be an erroneous conclusion. Our nets define what we shall catch.' It is almost certain to be the case that we will not discover through our testing system what levels of attainment pupils have reached in the more subtle and sophisticated dimensions of educational development. And the dangers are that we may decide either that they have not reached any worthwhile level in such dimensions or, more seriously – and more likely – that these are dimensions which do not matter. One notes here the recommendation of TGAT (DES, 1988a, para. 30) that 'assessment of attitudes should not form a prescribed part of the national assessment system'. And, while the report accepts that these should be included in records of achievement and that they 'might be considered by subject working groups in framing attainment targets' (ibid.), one must question the educational justification for, and the wisdom of, separating children's learning from their attitudes to learning. And one must recognize again that the backlash effect of this kind of narrow assessment on their educational experience will be a direct result of the quest for accuracy and thus of simplicity of goals.

This process can already be seen in the simplification of the attainment targets which has taken place. For, even where a working group has attempted to offer attainment targets of a more sophisticated kind, the process of simplification has been undertaken by the Secretary of State himself, and justified in terms of the need for accuracy. As we have seen, accuracy of assessment can be purchased only at the cost of those more complex dimensions of education which do not lend themselves to precise measurement – or even to measurement at all. Holistic assessment, for example, is an important dimension of the qualitative assessment of pupil capability, and there is clear evidence that this is, and must be, much more than an aggregation of individual measurements of performance. The national testing programme displays either an ignorance of this, perhaps self-evident, truth or a determination to turn the education system into something more limited and restricted – a training ground for industry, and, further, one based on inaccurate assessments of real capability.

Finally, we might note the reluctance already being shown by some schools and teachers to take in pupils identified as having special needs, in spite of the recommendations of the Warnock Report (DES, 1978a) that such pupils be taught in ordinary schools and classrooms wherever possible. Clearly this reluctance is based on an awareness that such pupils may require additional attention, and perhaps also resources, which must consequently reduce what can be devoted to achieving the highest possible test scores with the others. This is a further, and unfortunate, example of the backlash effect of the assessment system on the nature and quality of the experience offered to all pupils.

FACTORS LEADING TO UNDERACHIEVEMENT

The third main point at which we suggested the evidence of past attempts at national testing might offer insights into the likely effects of this new assessment programme is that of some of the reasons which have been offered for the inaccuracies of these tests and the underachievement of many pupils taking them.

To some extent of course these inaccuracies are due to attempts to assess the more complex kinds of educational achievement. But there is also massive evidence that 'success' or 'failure' at 11+ was determined to an unacceptable degree by extraneous factors and especially by socio-economic class, ethnic origin and gender.

First, we must note the kinds of irrelevant factor which the research evidence clearly indicated were playing their part in the assessment of pupils and their subsequent placement, both in streams at 7+ and in selective secondary schools at 11+. In particular, it is worth noting the effects of the date, specifically the month, of birth. The evidence clearly indicated that winter-born children fared better both at 7+ and 11+ than those born in summer; and, while there were those naïve enough to attribute this to the weather (in spite of the advent of domestic central heating), the more obvious and sensible reason was the length of time pupils had spent in full-time education. This could vary between two years for summer-born children and up to three years for those born in winter. Clearly this had to be a major feature – if a totally irrelevant and unacceptable one – of performance, especially at 7+.

The TGAT Report (DES, 1988a) recognizes the significance of factors such as this, but offers little to combat them beyond the advice that 'care should be taken at all reporting ages, but especially at this age [7+], to avoid giving the impression that the assessment is a predictor of future performance' (op. cit., para. 148). And this was presumably one reason why it recommended that assessment at seven+ should not be summative. However, as we have seen, that recommendation has already been overridden, and it may again be that we have a piece of advice which is unrealistic in relation to the inevitabilities of practice.

A second major influence on performance at both 7+ and 11+ which emerged from the research of the 1960s and 1970s was those important differences in children's rates of cognitive development – again especially significant at 7+. Extensive research into children's development has revealed, not surprisingly, that, just as they develop physically at different rates (not all of them producing their second teeth, for example, at the same age, or, later, reaching sexual maturity 'as a cohort'), so too they vary massively in the rates of their cognitive or intellectual development.

To assume, therefore, that all will be equally in a position to do themselves justice at the same time is to fly in the face of this kind of evidence. We noted in Chapter 3 some of the dangers of the use of metaphor; here we see evidence that if we think of children as born in cohorts, we are likely to envisage their progress through the education system as that of a cohort of Roman soldiers marching shoulder to shoulder up Watling Street. The reality is that differential rates of development will lead to differential levels of performance in tests, as all the evidence available to us indicates; and those differential levels of performance will reflect not ability, not potential, not even commitment, but the vagaries of maturation. Again, therefore, we have good reasons for not regarding assessment at these tender ages as summative or as 'a predictor of future performance' (DES, 1988a, para. 148). Again, however, we must note that in practice, however good these reasons are, these things will happen and many individual pupils will be inaccurately assessed, no matter how good the SATs, and thus ill served by the education system.

The third, and perhaps the most disturbing, of the factors identified as preventing pupils from doing themselves justice when in the past they have been tested at 7+ for allocation to streams or at 11+ for allocation to secondary schools is that of socio-economic background. This has been reinforced by similar evidence of performance in public examinations at 16+ (Douglas, Ross and Simpson, 1968). This evidence, it might also be noted, not only casts doubts on the potential validity of the new programme of national testing, it also emphasizes what was said in Chapter 3 about the fundamentally élitist nature and effects of the National Curriculum.

It must be acknowledged again that the TGAT Report (DES, 1988a) also recognizes that this will be a factor. However, its concern seems to focus on the implications of this for the overall performance of individual *schools*. 'It is well known', it tells us, 'that a variety of socio-economic factors so affect pupils' capacity to respond to school work that they can lead to very wide differences between the performances of different schools' (op. cit., para. 133). Its advice is not that we should attempt to scale the data to allow for such factors; this for a number of reasons it suggests would not work. Rather, the publishing of the results should be in the context of a wider report on the school and especially the socio-economic factors which may influence its work. 'Results should not be adjusted for socio-economic background but the report should include a general statement, prepared by the Local Authority for the area, of the nature and possible size of socio-economic and other influences which could affect schools in that area' (op. cit., para. 134).

This proposal may ease the problem for the schools themselves. It does little to ease it for the individual pupils whose achievements may be limited by factors of this kind and whose potential will thus not be revealed, or for their parents. Again we must note that this may present less difficulty in the context of assessment which is neither summative nor seen as 'a predictor of future performance' (op. cit., para. 148). Since these safeguards are unlikely to be maintained, however, to disregard the influence of such factors on the performance of individual pupils is tantamount to saying that they must be accepted and that there is nothing we can or should do about the many pupils whose progress will inevitably be held back in this way.

The evidence that this did happen as a result of earlier testing procedures, and for some of the reasons why it happened, is overwhelmingly convincing. Again there is not the scope here to explore this mass of evidence in detail. (And again one felt that it had long been accepted and had become a part of history.) Two very broad and general aspects of the evidence must be noted, however. The first of these is that a major factor in the manifest underachievement of pupils within these categories in test situations is the mismatch between the tests and their own background of values, attitudes, customs and, especially, language. Difficulties were created, for example, by the language of the tests for those pupils whose language is, because of social background, 'restricted'. And it is quite clear that pupils for whom English is a second language may not do themselves full justice in tests framed in English. This was apparent in the 11+ examinations of the past; it must also be true of the new testing programme. For bilingual children in the first or infant schools, for example, their bilingualism, which is seen by most teachers as a source of strength in relation to the development of their linguistic abilities – and thus their intellectual development – will become a positive disadvantage. It is to be noted that the likelihood of this is appreciated in respect of Welsh-speaking children and every effort is being made, at great additional expense, to develop appropriate and parallel test instruments in the Welsh language. Nothing comparable is being done in relation to pupils whose first, or second, language is other than English or Welsh.

Thus a major reason for underachievement in the past which is likely to be replicated in the new system is that of mismatch between social or ethnic background and the language and expectations built into the tests. There is thus an inherent potential for the re-emergence of many of those educational inequalities which have been revealed by earlier studies. And the failure, or unwillingness, to take account of these studies is further evidence of the élitist effects, and possibly intentions, of the new policies which we commented on in Chapter 3.

In this respect, we must also note the evidence, again gleaned from studies of the 11+ examination, that 'failure' breeds further failure and 'success' further success. Far from being spurred to greater effort by low scores, pupils who 'failed' the 11+, or who were allocated to a low stream at 7+, were shown to lower their sights immediately. It was plain, too, that their teachers reduced their own levels of expectation of these pupils, rather than working to raise their levels of attainment. In short, we had a 'self-fulfilling prophecy'. Once labelled 'below average', whether inaccurately or not, pupils tend to continue to produce below average performances, and their teachers to settle for such levels and to expect little more of them, so that the gaps in levels of performance between pupils in different streams or schools or categories of whatever kind become greater rather than smaller (Douglas, 1964).

One reason for this, of course, is that pupils who perform badly lose heart. In sporting cliché, their heads go down. They lose the interest and the motivation to continue to work at things they appear to be unable to succeed at – a particularly undesirable, and indeed unforgivable, experience to offer a seven-year-old.

This takes us to the second factor we need to note as contributing to an explanation of why pupils from certain kinds of background do badly in educational situations of this kind. For it is not only a matter of the nature of the exercises they are required to do; it is also, and more important, a matter of their response to those exercises, and, indeed, to the curriculum in its totality. In short, not only do some pupils lose heart when the evidence begins to appear that they are doing badly; some pupils are in fact doing badly because what they are required to do has been planned without reference to their social, ethnic or cultural background. And this is another source of that élitism to which we have so often referred. Some children must do badly, not through any lack of ability, intelligence, innate capacities or any other such quality we may wish to name, but because what they are offered is not designed to draw that ability out, to tap that intelligence, to develop those innate capacities.

This is a point which takes us beyond assessment and into the wider issues of pupils' response to the curriculum offered. We shall take up in the next chapter these and other aspects of empirical research and experience which have been ignored in the planning of the National Curriculum.

SUMMARY AND CONCLUSIONS

Before we consider these issues, however, let us summarize what it has been suggested the architects of the National Curriculum have failed to learn from previous experience and earlier studies of educational assessment. There is no evidence of any recognition of the dangers and disadvantages of an assessment-led curriculum, of the inherent inaccuracies of any assessment scheme which attempts to go beyond the most simplistic kinds of attainment, of the consequent backlash effect on to the curriculum which takes the form of emphasizing those simplistic attainments at the expense of more sophisticated, and valuable, educational experiences, and of the many factors, especially those of a social, ethnic and cultural kind, which influence pupils' test performances and must lead to, or aggravate, those élitist features which we have already noted a subject-based and centrally determined and controlled curriculum must evince.

Nor are there grounds for assuming, or even hoping, that the influence of these factors may have diminished in the intervening years. Indeed, there is every reason to conjecture that, with the additional complexity of multi-ethnicity, they may well have come to loom even larger.

We must of course allow for the possibility that these disadvantages which have been detected in all previous attempts at national or public assessment, both in this country and elsewhere, will be counteracted in the new testing procedures; that the standard assessment tasks developed will justify the large sums of money expended on them and will break new ground in educational assessment; and that the task which the TGAT Report set us, 'to devise such a system afresh' (DES, 1988a, para. 13), will be successfully accomplished. It does, however, seem somewhat irresponsible to plan a national system of curriculum and assessment on the assumption that someone is likely to invent a form of pupil assessment of a kind that the world has never seen before, especially when all known and available evidence seems to suggest that such a system is a logical and human impossibility. It is rather like planning the national health service on the premise that the passing of a law which requires it will ensure the immediate discovery of a complete cure for cancer. As Desmond Nuttall (1988, p. 65) has said, 'a massive research and development exercise is required, and in many cases will have to solve as yet unsolved problems in educational measurement'.

Nor do the paragraphs in which the TGAT Report attempts to allay the fears of those who 'are deeply opposed to any system of national assessment and testing' (DES, 1988a, para. 13) do much to reassure such persons. For those paragraphs take a very narrow view of what it is that prompts such fears and leads some to be deeply opposed to the system. They do not, for example, make any reference to the studies we have mentioned earlier in this section or to the kinds of fears and concerns we have seen they generate. And to refer, as the report does, to graded assessment schemes as examples of what assessment and testing when 'carefully aligned to the curriculum' (op. cit., para. 14) can do to enhance pupil motivation is to compound rather than to dispel the problem we noted earlier of simplistic views of and approaches to learning. No doubt pupils can be motivated by graded assessment schemes to proceed effectively along a linear path to increased assimilation of knowledge. And if that were all there were to education, we need look no further in our planning of it than the work of the behavioural psychologists and to their teaching machines (which would, and perhaps now will, very soon replace the – increasingly in short supply – teachers). However, the main concern about national assessment which was expressed above was precisely that education should be seen as encapsulating far more than that, and that a national system of assessment such as that with which we are now presented makes it more difficult, and perhaps impossible, for it to do so. One has to concede that in its attempts to allay such fears the TGAT Report was operating within its own concept of a national assessment system which, as we saw earlier, was a system which was to be formative and diagnostic but not summative (except at 16+). It is the summative dimension which compounds one's fears and diminishes, almost to the point of total non-validity, the attempts of the TGAT Report to dispel them.

The last substantive point we made about the national assessment programme was that, on past evidence, it is most likely to reinforce those other élitist features of the new policies we have noted, especially as a result of the likely response of pupils, or at least of pupils from certain kinds of background, to it. The next chapter, then, is devoted to a consideration of what this evidence indicates we should expect on this front.

5
THE NATIONAL CURRICULUM – AN EMPIRICAL EVALUATION II: OTHER RESEARCH EVIDENCE

It was indicated at the beginning of Chapter 4 why it is important to explore how far the planning and implementation of the National Curriculum have taken account of knowledge and experience we already possess in major areas of relevance to curriculum planning of any kind and at any level. That chapter also proceeded to demonstrate not only the failure to do that in relation to the associated programme of assessment and testing but also some of the likely results and consequences of that failure.

We also identified there several other major areas in which similar short-comings might be detected. First, it was suggested that insufficient attention had been paid to the evidence we have of how pupils learn, what motivates them and how they respond to certain teaching approaches and forms of curriculum. Second, it was claimed that little concern had been shown for recent developments in our understanding of the education of pupils with special needs. Third, it was asserted that there has been a similar lack of recognition of what we have learned about the role of the teacher in the educational process. And, finally, it was suggested that experience and knowledge of the problems of the dissemination of curriculum change and innovation, and especially of the impracticability of attempts to control the curriculum from outside the school, had also been ignored in the planning of the new system.

All these claims must now be explored in greater detail.

PUPIL RESPONSE

Children's minds

We have commented on several occasions on the problems created by the subject base of the National Curriculum, the fact that it is planned by reference primarily to subjects and their recommended content rather than from a proper concern with, or understanding of, the pupils who are to be the recipients of its offerings. This is very much a traditional way of planning educational provision, as we have suggested elsewhere, and it is one which was roundly criticized by Jean-Jacques Rousseau as long ago as 1762: 'The wisest writers devote themselves to what a man ought to know, without asking what a child is capable of learning.' It may of course be argued that the subject working groups are doing just that, but such an argument would be placing a very simplistic interpretation on Rousseau's words. For he was not suggesting that we should decide what children need to learn to become adults and parcel it up into pieces they can handle, chunk by chunk; he was going much further than that and suggesting that we should select their educational diet by reference to what he called their 'childish interests' rather than to the subjects we as adults feel they ought to learn – whatever the reasons for our choices. We should not do what Rousseau says most educationists do, who are 'always looking for the man in the child, without considering what he is before he becomes a man'. Childhood is more than a time of preparation for adulthood. And we must respect what Charles Dickens once called 'the childhood of the mind', and accept his warning against the possibilities of injuring this.

Rousseau's work, for reasons which will be readily apparent, gave great impetus to the study of child psychology. One branch of this, that known as behaviourism, has indeed concentrated on methods of teaching and learning, mostly through experiments with animals; and its findings would support and contribute to that narrower view of education which sees the main task as being little more than that of finding the most efficient methods of ensuring that pupils learn what it has been decided they should learn.

The second main branch of educational or child psychology, the developmental school, has, through the work of such people as Jean Piaget and, more recently, Jerome Bruner and others, explored the nature of children's minds and attempted to reach a more subtle view of the learning process, not as a mechanistic device for acquiring 'skills, knowledge and understanding' but as a process of intellectual development. And the work of this school has led to a concept of teaching not as a matter of merely offering the right stimuli to bring about the desired learning responses, but as providing the environment and the experiences which will promote intellectual development in its widest sense.

Clearly, these two schools lend their support to two quite different kinds of educational ideology, and to two quite different conceptions of the curriculum; and it is not the intention here either to explore these differences (not least since we did this to some extent in Chapter 3) or to fudge our present task by offering the one as evidence to confute the other. It is enough that we recognize that to adopt a content-based, linear view of teaching and learning is to have rejected as largely irrelevant the insights offered by studies of child development.

Some of those studies, however, do have relevance for how children, and especially young children, learn, whatever form of educational provision one is attempting to expose them to. And so to ignore these aspects of such studies is again to refuse to acknowledge evidence that is highly pertinent to any form of educational planning. Several aspects of the understanding of intellectual development which have emerged from these studies are important to note here as having been largely ignored by those planning the National Curriculum.

The early work of Piaget and his associates led to the view that there are important qualitative differences in the intellectual functioning of the child compared to that of the developed adult, that children are not mini-adults, to educate whom we need to do no more than express things in simple terms; they actually view the world and respond to it in a quite different way. To educate children, then, and to help them on to further stages of intellectual development, we must understand the main features of their forms of cognitive functioning.

Recent studies have elaborated on this theme and have suggested that the differences one can detect in kinds and levels of cognitive functioning are not stages, as Piaget thought, which as we develop we leave behind, but rather forms of representation (Eisner, 1982) and understanding which persist into adulthood, different strategies – such as the enactive, the iconic and the symbolic (Bruner, 1968) – for understanding the world, thinking about it and manipulating it. Hence to be fully educated, or fully developed intellectually, it is necessary not for one to have learnt, step by step, certain subjects, but to have acquired all possible strategies for handling effectively the elements in one's environment in order to have gained maximum control over one's destiny. On this evidence, then, the prime concern of education is not the acquisition of bodies of knowledge, although that clearly is an important part of things, but what has been called 'the growth of competence'.

Second, these studies have revealed that this 'growth of competence' is not to be brought about by even the most careful and painstakingly structured instruction in school subjects. It requires what has been called 'active learning', an active engagement (not of course necessarily physical) with the substance of one's learning. Educational experiences must be real experiences, genuinely personal and significant to the learner, since they must be assimilated by the learner and accommodated to his or her existing cognitive structures.

Hence, third, such experiences must not be decontextualized or disembedded; they must at least begin in a recognizable and meaningful context (although of course a major task for the teacher is to take the pupil beyond that immediate context). As an example of this we might cite Martin Hughes's work on the mathematical development of young children. For he asserts that 'the formal code of arithmetic contains a number of features which distinguish it from the informal mathematics which children acquire before school' (Hughes, 1986, p. 168), so that children who know very well that two bricks and two bricks make four bricks have great difficulty with the formal, abstract, disembedded, decontextualized assertion that 'two and two make four' or, worse, '2 + 2 = 4'. They thus need help to build links between their informal and formal understandings, and those links must begin with and be contextualized or embedded in the former.

There are no doubt messages here for those planning to teach the subjects of the National Curriculum to young children. It would seem unlikely, however, that these are messages which can be held in view at all stages of such teaching, or that pupils in the early years of education can, in the context of subject-based and linear programmes of study, be given the kinds of experience that these studies suggest they need if they are to develop to the fullest extent their intellectual capacities. It seems especially unlikely that these insights can be reflected in the assessment of their levels of performance at 7+, not least because there is a conflict between these views of learning and the notion of 'correct' answers which is likely to be an essential feature of any system of national attainment testing.

Two further aspects of this work are also worthy of note. The first is the impossibility, within the context of this kind of approach to education, of separating out the affective from the cognitive dimensions of children's experience. Both must play their parts in parallel in the development of forms of representation or understanding, and it must be recognized that both will be important parts of any experiences which satisfy the criteria we have just considered. It has been claimed (Eisner, 1982) that traditional forms of education in the Western world have discounted the affective aspects of experience and have thus been limited and diminished in that they have ignored a number of the forms of representation he has posited as essential to full cognitive functioning. Yet it must be pointed out that it is exactly those affective aspects of education which are at risk in a curriculum whose core consists of technologically useful subjects, which is fundamentally instrumental and which is to be assessed by forms of testing that are likely to emphasize the more simplistic and readily measurable aspects of learning.

Finally, we must note the evidence which has emerged from these studies of the importance of the social context to human learning, growth and development.

The forms of representation which it is claimed human beings need to develop in order to function at maximum efficiency are public forms of representation; they are the means of gaining access to public structures through which the meanings of experience are not merely internalized but are also shared. Culture is not merely a body of knowledge from which we select the content of our curriculum; it is the totality of the environment in which the child lives and with which education should help him or her to come to terms in order to operate effectively within that cultural milieu.

Human beings, then, are from birth socio-centric. Bruner and Haste (1987, p. 1) have described the effects of these studies as 'a quiet revolution', and they have further said of it: 'It is not only that we have begun to think again of the child as a *social being* . . . but because we have come once more to appreciate that through such social life, the child acquires a framework for interpreting experience, and learns how to negotiate meaning in a manner congruent with the requirements of the culture. ''Making sense'' is a social process' (ibid.).

All the research evidence, then, points to the fact that from birth children are attempting to engage actively with their environment in order to develop public forms of understanding and representation, that this engagement involves the senses as well as the intellect and that a central feature of that environment is the other human beings within it. This offers us a view of education as a far more sophisticated process than that envisaged by the planners of the National Curriculum. For the model of learning which emerges from the 1988 Act itself and from all its supporting documentation not only, as we have seen, stresses the linearity of the learning process and largely ignores its affective dimensions, it also reveals no awareness of the importance of the social dimension. It is a factory-farming model of learning in which each child, like a battery hen, is to assimilate as much as possible of the food offered to it. There is no allowance, except at the methodological level, for the individual nature of each child's learning style. The diet of all is to be the same. Only the dosage is to vary, since the only forms of individualism acknowledged are those of ability and of rates of assimilation of the diet – the individualism of behavioural psychology from which the research we have just briefly noted has been leading educationists away for more than twenty years.

Nor, as was suggested at the beginning, is this only a matter of competing ideologies. Many of the insights offered by developmental psychology are of a kind that demand attention in any educational planning, whatever its ideological perspective. For, if this is how children learn, then, whatever our ideology, we must allow for it in our planning. This has clearly not been done by the architects of the National Curriculum, which is, as a result, flawed in several major ways in relation to what it requires of teachers and children, especially in the early years of schooling. One wonders what Prince Charles's view is of architects who begin to design and build their edifices from the top rather than from the foundations.

The likely response of young children to what the National Curriculum and its testing programme require of them can perhaps be gauged from the evidence of the studies we have just referred to and many other related researches. The suggestion is that children are unlikely to gain much that is of lasting value from what they are to be offered, that, further, their response to it may not be that which is desired, and that it might have been of advantage to its planners to have paid some heed to the messages emerging from these sources (even though these would not have been supportive of what they clearly intended to bring about and might have revealed to them its impracticability).

There is, however, another body of evidence which we must consider which concerns the likely reactions of pupils at the other end of the age range to a curriculum which has been framed by reference to its subjects and their content rather than in relation to potential pupil reaction. It is to this that we now turn.

Alienation

A major factor in that failure of many pupils to take advantage of educational opportunities which we noted in Chapter 4, their failure to do themselves justice in public tests and examinations and their resultant underachievement, has clearly been the mismatch between the content of the curriculum they have been offered and their own values and interests. This mismatch has led to a low level of motivation, in some cases a sense of alienation, a feeling that their own preoccupations were being ignored, devalued, dismissed and even demeaned by the system, and a consequent rejection of that system. It is well authenticated that this progressively worsening state has led not only to underachievement on the part of such pupils but also to disaffection, to truancy and absenteeism, and to disruptive behaviour both inside and outside schools. For the attitudes of the school system have been – not unreasonably – seen as the attitudes of society itself, and the alienation has been social as well as educational.

Underachievement on a quite massive scale was first identified in the research undertaken for the report on *Early Leaving* (CACE, 1954). These findings were reinforced by the studies of the Crowther Committee (CACE, 1959). Both studies revealed that an unacceptable proportion of very able pupils was leaving school with little or nothing in the form of qualifications to show for the time spent there. Similar evidence was emerging at the same time in the USA. And the factors most obviously associated with this underachievement on both sides of the Atlantic were socio-economic and ethnic background. These underachieving pupils were of working-class origin or black, or both. (At that time the British evidence related mainly to working-class pupils and that from the USA to black pupils.)

The existence of national service in the United Kingdom in the 1950s enabled accurate surveys to be made of the eighteen-to-twenty-year-old population, and such a survey undertaken on behalf of the Crowther Committee revealed that, while in the population as a whole 9 per cent of the top ability group had left school at fifteen with no qualifications, the figure for the sons of unskilled manual workers was 28 per cent, with those of skilled and semi-skilled manual workers not far behind; and of the second level of ability the overall figure was 65 per cent, with 86, 77 and 73 per cent respectively for the three groups of manual workers (CACE, 1959).

These findings were clearly very disturbing – even to those whose view of education was confined to Crowther's notion of education as a national invest-ment. For they indicated not only that pupils from certain kinds of background were being personally disadvantaged, but also that the country was failing fully to develop a major resource: the natural talent of its people. Hence a great deal of attention was devoted to attempting to identify the causes of this state of affairs, with a view to correcting it.

Much of that attention was originally directed at the homes of these pupils. 'Deficiencies' were identified in working-class and black families which were contributing to the 'failure' of their offspring in schools, 'deficiencies' like those language 'deficiencies' we referred to in Chapter 4. It quickly became apparent, however, that what were being peceived as 'deficiencies' in the home were being aggravated by major features of the school system – in particular, again as we saw in Chapter 4, streaming, especially in the primary schools, and the 11+ selection procedures. Steps were thus taken, as we also noted there, to eliminate, or at least to minimize, the effects of such factors.

However, it slowly became clear that even the abolition of streaming and of the 11+ selection procedures would achieve little if the central cause were not addressed. Testing and selection play their part and, as we have seen, that is a major part, in promoting the underachievement of large groups of pupils and thus militating against the attainment of a fair and egalitarian system of education. By far the major cause, however, is the curriculum itself.

As has become apparent from many studies over the last two decades, the curriculum reflects the values of those who design and plan it. And, if those values are the values neither of those who are expected to receive that curriculum nor of their parents, their peers and their culture, that curriculum will not be accepted and many such pupils will feel only a sense of alienation from it – and from the society which is thrusting it upon them. In the language of the develop-mental psychologists we noted earlier, they will not assimilate it because they cannot accommodate it; it cannot lead to the kind of active and experiential learning which they would claim is the only true form of learning, and certainly the only route to a proper form of intellectual development; and it does not assist the individual to come to terms with his or her cultural environment in order to operate effectively within it. There is no negotiation of meanings. Such a curriculum is a one-way process, when a two-way transaction is necessary for educational advance.

Hence many such pupils have rejected what has been offered as reflecting an alien, and alienating, culture, a set of values in conflict with their own and those of their parents, and even as attempting to devalue their culture and their values as in some sense inferior, and to impose a different culture and a different set of values on them, with all the overtones of social control that this implies.

As a result, many attempts have been made in recent years to tackle this problem, or this set of problems, through modifications to and adaptations of the curriculum. The content of the curriculum has been recognized as being problematic and, indeed, as being the source of these difficulties. In many areas the concept of curriculum negotiation has been accepted and working from the interests of the pupils themselves has been advocated. This has been a major factor in the emergence of that view of curriculum as process which we noted in Chapter 3. For it has been recognized that, if the enhancement of the individual's powers, capacities and control over his or her environment is what education is about, then the content of that individual's educational experience can and must be adjusted to his or her individual background and needs. To use the example we gave in Chapter 3, history can as well be taught, or rather the development of historical understanding can as well be promoted, through the study of Mogul India as through that of Tudor England.

Indeed, the DES itself indicated its recognition of this problem, and moreover its acceptance of this solution, in its reply to the report, *The West Indian Community*, by the Select Committee on Race Relations and Immigration (1977). For in that reply it asserted: 'For the curriculum to have meaning and relevance for all pupils now in our schools, its content, emphasis and the values and assumptions contained must reflect the wide range of cultures, histories and life styles in our multiracial society' (DES, 1978b, para. 38). The current abandonment of that stance is another example of that dramatic change of direction – and, indeed, loss of understanding – by the DES and HMI which we have noted on several occasions.

It is not the concern here, however, to explore all the many curriculum changes which have been prompted by a desire to deal with this problem of alienation, disaffection, underachievement and consequent inequality and injustice. It is enough to draw attention to the fact that, here again, there are important lessons, supported by massive evidence, which have been ignored by the planners of the National Curriculum. For its base, as we have seen so often, is essentially a list of subjects, whether these are to be taught as subjects or not; and these subjects are defined clearly in terms of quite specific content; and that content is manifestly intended to reflect one set of values and not several, since it must have 'sufficient in common to enable children to move from one area of the country to another with minimum disruption to their education' (DES, 1987, p. 4) – a very odd basis on which to plan the education of all children; and those values are inevitably those of the planners.This emerges perhaps most starkly in the report of the National Curriculum History Working Group, whose chairman's supplementary guidance included the advice that:

> The programmes of study should have at the core the history of Britain, the record of its past and, in particular, its political, constitutional and cultural heritage. They should also take account of Britain's evolution and its changing role as a European, Commonwealth and world power influencing and being influenced by ideas, movements and events elsewhere in the world.
>
> (DES, 1989e, pp. 15–16 and 105)

The report goes on to say that

> individual people in these islands have much in common but they also have many individual characteristics specific to country, ethnic grouping, religion, gender and social class. We do not believe that school history can be so finely-tuned as to accommodate all these details all the time, but at least it can make pupils aware of the richness and variety of British culture and its historical origins.
>
> (op. cit., p. 17)

The unilateral view of 'British culture' is plain from that quotation, which merely nods in the direction of cultural pluralism without demonstrating any understanding of what that implies for educational provision or curriculum planning. And the fine-tuning which the report asserts is not possible is indeed not possible in the context of the narrow, content-based conception of curriculum within which it is working and beyond which it seems incapable of seeing. Fine-tuning would require a more sophisticated curriculum model, as we have seen on so many occasions.

History is the school subject *par excellence* in which one can recognize the value component, in which one can detect most readily the values of the planners. These may be less obvious in other subjects, but they are none the less there. And these values are quickly recognized – if not explicitly then intuitively – by pupils, especially when they are in conflict with their own cultural values, and the result is that alienation which has been well documented over the last several decades.

Again, therefore, we have a body of evidence, of understanding, of insights which has enormous relevance and significance for curriculum planning and which has apparently been ignored or rejected by the architects of the National Curriculum.

One further point must be made which follows naturally from this discussion. We have heard much in recent years of the 'hidden' curriculum. It has been made very apparent that pupils learn far more at school than is stated in the official curriculum, no matter how detailed that might be. Every aspect of every curriculum is value laden – the choice of subjects, the choice of content, the choice of aims, the choice of models and approaches. And those values are communicated to the recipients of that curriculum in very subtle ways.

An awareness of this makes it incumbent on those planning a curriculum to be alive to the values which underpin and are reflected in it and to the 'hidden' learning it will promote. It is not enough to say that, because it is hidden, it is not the planners' responsibility. It is the direct result of the planners' work and they must take full responsibility for it.

Again, however, one sees little evidence that this has been acknowledged or even recognized by those who have planned the National Curriculum. We have seen that the values of that curriculum are instrumentalism, commercialism, competition and élitism. We have seen that it offers a view of society which pays little heed to the quality of life but devotes all its attention and energies to the means of living. We have noted that it pays little attention and offers little respect to cultural differences. We have seen that it accepts a form of élitism, or at least adopts a limited concept of equality as equality of access and opportunity only, and that it appears to accept no responsibility for, certainly it includes no plans for, those who do not succeed by the standards which it has set up.

These, then, are some of the values implicit in the National Curriculum, and these, on all known evidence, will form its 'hidden' aspects. These are the attitudes and values which pupils are likely to pick up as a by-product of the curriculum with which they are being presented.

Again, it may well be that this is recognized and accepted by those who have planned this curriculum. Certainly these are the values which they themselves seem to embrace and advocate. If this is the case, we can merely acknowledge that these are their values and that it is their view that their electoral mandate entitles them to assume that they are the majority values and thus to impose them on the child population. However, we should perhaps note John White's claim (White *et al.*, 1981, p. 15) that it is not the case that '*any* government is entitled to pronounce on aims and curricula, but only a government committed to the principles of democracy'. And we might in any case wish to challenge the right of any group within society to impose any one set of values through the education system, whatever those values happen to be. Further, at the very least, it is incumbent upon anyone acting in this way to make clear that this is his or her intention, so that everyone can be left in no doubt about what at root the policy is. If, on the other hand, this is not the intention, then, since it is certainly the effect, again we have an example of a major area of understanding being ignored in the planning of the National Curriculum, again with the result that effects will follow from it which could have been foreseen if the trouble had been taken to take note of evidence already available.

PUPILS WITH SPECIAL NEEDS

Another very important group of pupils, whose needs must be taken very seriously and for whom the making of appropriate provision must loom very large in
the planning of any curriculum whose real, and not merely stated, concern is with
raising the quality of educational experiences for all pupils, is that large group of
pupils deemed to have special educational needs. We noted in Chapter 1 that the
Warnock Report (DES, 1978a) had suggested that as many as 20 per cent of
pupils will at some stage during their education have special needs in the sense
that the report gave to the term, so that only in the strictly mathematical sense is
this a minority group, since in real, and moral, terms it is a very significant
minority (as, indeed, it would be even if it were much smaller). Yet, as we also
noted in Chapter 1, the reference in the 1988 Act to this group and to its many
needs is very brief and amounts to little more than permission for such children to
be offered a modified version of the National Curriculum, or, in extreme cases, to
be exempted from it altogether. (One is tempted to comment here that for the first
time in the history of education in England and Wales such children may thus be
positively advantaged in relation to their less fortunate peers, for whom no such
exemption is possible.)

We also noted in Chapter 1 the subsequent elucidation of what such modification or 'disapplication' might mean which has been provided by the DES in
National Curriculum: From Policy to Practice (DES, 1989c). We saw, for example, that the assumption has been made that all pupils will be able to make
some progress with the National Curriculum, that the freedom teachers have to
adjust their methods and approaches is felt to go some way toward dealing with
the problem, that it is even being suggested that such pupils might be taught in
mixed-age classes, by which one infers that they might be 'kept down' as their
more 'normal' colleagues and peers move up through the system, and that, only if
all these devices fail, will arrangements for modification, adaptation, disapplication and/or exemption come into play.

This is an aspect of the National Curriculum which has already attracted a
good deal of critical comment. Not the least reason for this is that over the last
decade or so much attention has been given to the issue of pupils with special
needs, most notably through the work of the Warnock Committee (DES, 1978a)
and the consequent legislation of the 1981 Education Act. And the general
reaction to the 1988 Act from those who understand the needs of such pupils
from the inside, as expressed, for example, by Klaus Wedell (1988, p. 111), is
that 'the passing of the 1981 Act represented the beginning of a statutory commitment to meeting their needs which the Education Reform Bill as presented to
Parliament has done nothing to confirm'.

It is not the intention here to reproduce or reiterate the criticisms which others have made of this aspect of the National Curriculum. Several points must be made, however, in the context of the more general critique being offered here. The first two of these stem from what seems to be the basic principle of the treatment of pupils with special needs within the National Curriculum, namely the assumption that all kinds of special need have the same effect in that they retard the progress of pupils through the linear, 'Thirty-Nine Steps' hierarchy of educational development, so that all one needs to do to take account of their needs is to allow for their slower rate of progress, and, if or when it is so slow as not to constitute progress at all, to exempt or excuse them from taking part in the race. First, there is no understanding or conception here that a curriculum might be conceived in terms different from that of the 'Thirty-Nine Steps' model – a point we explored in some detail in Chapter 3 – so that there is no understanding or conception of the fact that pupils with special needs might require a different kind of curriculum from that which the National Curriculum offers, and not merely a different pace, rate or mode of 'delivery'. The aims of education must be the same for all pupils, but, as we have noted already on several occasions, the operationalizing of those aims may take many forms and not only – perhaps not ever – the linear, hierarchical form offered by the National Curriculum.

And, second, this weakness not only stems from a lack of awareness of conceptual issues of curriculum (and/or that unwillingness to acknowledge the existence of valid alternative concepts of curriculum which we also noted in Chapter 3), but also reflects a failure to take any account of what has been learnt about the provision of education for pupils with special needs from both the experience and the research of many years, and in particular from the work that has been undertaken in the last decade or so, since the publication of the Warnock Report in 1978. There is in particular a failure to take account of the importance of the social context of learning. This, as we saw earlier, is a crucial factor in the educational growth and development of all children. To suggest that pupils with special educational needs might best be able to assimilate the National Curriculum if assigned to mixed-age classes, and thus presumably to work with pupils whose chronological age is much lower than their own, is not only to demonstrate yet again a philosophy which regards the curriculum as more important than its recipients, it is also to ignore completely the importance of the social context to all children's learning and development. It is also to cut across the policy of integrating such pupils in ordinary classrooms, which was strongly advocated by the Warnock Report (DES, 1978a), and to ignore all that have been learnt by those who have been endeavouring to implement that policy and/or to study both its effects and the practicalities of its implementation during the last decade. And it is to lose sight of the importance of personal and social education for all pupils and of the fact that this cannot be attained simply by close attention to subject studies and their content. In this context it is worth noting that *redoublement*, the practice of requiring pupils to repeat a year, 'has proved so undesirable in France and Germany' (Lawton, 1989a, p. 14), and that it was abolished – at least officially – in France in the 1960s, although it continues to be practised as an apparently unavoidable solution to the problem of steering pupils through the objectives, the 'Thirty-Nine Steps', of the French national curriculum (Gipps, 1988).

It must further be noted that arrangements for modification or disapplication apply only to those pupils who are the subjects of 'statements' made under section 7 of the 1981 Act. Yet these represent only a small proportion of that 20 per cent of pupils which the Warnock Report suggested would need special educational provision at some stage in their schooling. The planned arrangements, therefore, will not meet the needs of large numbers of pupils who, if the Warnock Committee was right, will require special provision of some kind and at some stage, 'the 18 per cent or so of children with special educational needs in ordinary schools without Statements' (Wedell, 1988, p. 104). Thus no account has been taken either of the changed concept of educational need which has emerged as a result of the Warnock Report or of the changes in educational practice and provision for pupils with special needs to which that change of concept has led.

Again, therefore, we have a set of policies which not only ignore but also fly in the face of available evidence, which place political interest before practical wisdom, and whose effect will be to set back those advances which have been made in recent years in both the principles and the practice of education for pupils with special educational needs. And so again we must note the intellectual impoverishment and/or the morally questionable ideology of the new policies.

THE ROLE OF THE TEACHER

We have considered in some detail many of the areas where research into and experience of the response of pupils to education have a relevance for, and should have been given more prominence in, the planning of the National Curriculum. Let us now turn to a brief consideration of what is known about the role of the teacher in the educational process.

It is quite plain that current policies change that role significantly. Teachers in England and Wales have long had a degree of freedom and control in curriculum matters which their colleagues in most other countries have not shared. That freedom and control have now been taken from them; control of the curriculum has been shifted to central government; and teachers are left with freedom and discretion only in the area of methodology, decisions about how to 'deliver' a curriculum whose nature and content have been determined elsewhere, and in relation to whatever, relatively very small, elements the curriculum might contain which do not fall within the prescribed foundation subjects, i.e. within the

National Curriculum, or within the basic curriculum (the National Curriculum and religious education).

The loss of this freedom and the consequent narrowing of professional scope have removed a good deal of the job satisfaction which brought many teachers into the profession and kept them there despite relatively low salaries. It is clearly a factor in the recent increase in early retirements from the profession and the consequent teacher shortage which has led to reduced staffing levels in many schools and sometimes to closures and/or part-closures. Salary levels clearly play their part in this, as do the conditions under which many teachers find themselves working. But the fall which is evident in teacher morale is at least as much a result of the undermining of their professionalism and the reduction in their scope for exercising their professional judgement which the introduction of the National Curriculum, and especially the planning of it with little reference to the teachers, have brought about.

That in itself constitutes a major criticism of these policies, but, since it is manifestly the intention of those policies to reduce teacher autonomy and to increase external control over them, it is not a criticism which the proponents of those policies would accept, and, as was indicated in the introduction, it is not the purpose of this book merely to disagree with, and to express dissatisfaction with, these policies.

What is relevant here and germane to our theme is that again we have an example of complete disregard of significant research evidence. For again there is massive evidence in support of the fact that the teacher's role is central and crucial to effective education, that the quality of education any pupil receives will depend to a very large extent on the quality of his or her teachers. And this quality is not merely a matter of teaching ability, of skill in transmitting subject knowledge, but goes far beyond that to the making of those professional judgements which are essential to promoting the educational development of pupils. Those professional judgements, however, can be made by teachers only if they have the scope and freedom to act on them, or at least they can be of value to their pupils only if they can be acted on. Where that freedom is considerably restricted, as it is in the context of a prescribed national curriculum which offers scope only for judgements about effective methods of 'delivery', and reduces the role of the teacher to that of a technician, 'a carrier of knowledge with transmission skills' (Goddard, 1985, p. 35), the potential for the educational development of pupils must also be diminished. *Teaching* can be conducted by remote control; *education* requires the interaction of individual pupil with individual teacher not only in an atmosphere of mutual trust and confidence but in a context which offers scope for such interaction to flourish and develop.

Again, therefore, the message is one of a weight of evidence and understanding having been ignored to the detriment of the quality of what is being offered and of the potential for genuine educational advance. The National Curriculum may achieve its aim of raising standards but it is unlikely that these will be standards of education.

A further area in which the evidence indicates that the teacher's role is crucial is that of the dissemination of curriculum innovation and change, and we must finally turn to an exploration of what this evidence has revealed.

THE DISSEMINATION OF INNOVATION AND CHANGE

It is clearly important that, to be effective, any change must ' "take" with the school and become fully institutionalised' (Hoyle, 1969, p. 230). 'The central problem . . . is the avoidance of tissue rejection whereby an innovation does not "take" with a school because the social system of the school is unable to absorb it into its normal functioning' (op. cit., p. 231). We have learnt a good deal about the mechanics and strategies of curriculum change in the years since Eric Hoyle drew our attention to that problem. Most importantly, the experience of many of the Schools Council's projects, in their attempts to introduce innovations into the school curriculum, led slowly but inexorably to an awareness of the centrality of the teacher to the effectiveness of such exercises. Its original use of what came to be called 'centre–periphery' models of dissemination, the development of a curriculum package at some central point and its dissemination to schools at some distance from that point, proved largely ineffective in bringing about genuine change, so that, in its later years, the Council accepted that effective curriculum development must be school-based and attempted to direct its energies and resources into supporting attempts by individual schools or groups of schools to develop their own curricula. There is clearly a lesson here which again has not been learnt by the planners of the National Curriculum, who appear to have given little or no attention to the strategies by which that curriculum might be most effectively implemented. For, 'here it is again, the old centre–periphery model, now reinforced with statutory concrete, ready for the relaunch' (Simons, 1988, p. 82). Again we seem to have an example of the assumption that passing a law will change the real world in ways hitherto unknown. Yet some of the reasons for the failure of centre–periphery approaches in the past would seem to apply even when such approaches have the added advantage (if advantage it be) of the force of law, and, perhaps more so, when the basic philosophy and import of the planned changes are likely to be far less congenial to most teachers than were those of the Schools Council's projects.

These reasons include the wide gap between the idea of the curriculum held by its central planners and that of the teachers attempting to implement it in their classrooms – a gap which has been shown to exist not only when the attempt has been to offer teachers a 'teacher-proof' blueprint, as with the National Curriculum, but even when every effort has been made to involve teachers in the actual planning or to explain to them the thinking behind the proposed change and the theoretical considerations underlying it in such a way as to try to ensure that these were fully understood and thus might be reflected in their practice. It is naïve, therefore, to assume, again as in the implementation of the National Curriculum, that short bursts of in-service training or the publication of documentation by NCC will resolve this difficulty.

Second, it is clear from the evidence that attempts at innovation do not work if the teacher is seen, and is treated, as a largely passive recipient of change and innovation planned on his or her behalf by others, whether professionals or amateurs. In these circumstances, teachers have often been seen to 'cannibalize' what they have been offered, to modify it and adapt it to the particular context of their own teaching and to the norms of their own group. They have even been known to sabotage such schemes. Teacher-proof curricula were shown long ago to be unworkable; and 'the teacher-proof packaged curriculum . . . was tested to destruction in the first wave of post-war curriculum reform' (Simons, 1988, p. 82).

Third, teachers need to be, or to become, committed to any planned change if it is to work. The motivation of teachers to make it work is crucial, not least because any change, and especially change as far-reaching as the implementation of the National Curriculum, requires that they be prepared to put in much extra work. And there is much evidence to show that teachers tend to be so motivated only if they are involved in what is happening and, indeed, to some extent in control, if they have been consulted in, or have been party to, the planning of the change, or if they have been aware of the need for change and recognize what is proposed as meeting that need, as extending 'the range of their strategies for dealing with the problem' (MacDonald and Rudduck, 1971, pp. 150–1).

None of these conditions would seem to apply in the implementation of the National Curriculum, so that again one is surprised to see that no allowance seems to have been made for them, no acknowledgement taken of the existence of these difficulties and no provision or strategies for implementation other than the passing of a law, the provision of in-service facilities and a plethora of pamphlets.

> Twenty-five years of sustained and systematic effort to improve the educational quality of schooling, especially the quality of secondary schooling for all, have generated, cumulatively and often painfully, a body of experienced-based learning about the limitations of social engineering and some promising alternative paths to improvement. This learning is notable by its complete absence from Government thinking.
>
> (Simons, 1988, p. 82)

The distinction has long been made between the 'official' curriculum and the 'actual', the 'planned' and the 'received'. This distinction reflects a well-known phenomenon, namely that there is always a gap between the intentions of the planners and the realities of attempts to implement those intentions, even when such attempts are sincere and strenuous. It has long been recognized that the major problem of curriculum development, and, indeed, of educational advance, is the closing of this gap, and, further, that the teacher is the key figure in this process. To assume it can be closed by legislation is naïve. To expect to close it by the provision of 'Baker days' is simplistic. To ignore it in the planning of a national curriculum is irresponsible.

Furthermore, there is positive evidence from recent experience of the success which can be achieved when there is full and proper involvement of teachers in the development of the curriculum. The successes of the GCSE are in large measure attributable to the involvement of teachers both in the overall decision-making processes and in the interpretation of these general decisions in the context of their own classrooms and schools. And it must be acknowledged that, despite its inauspicious beginnings and largely instrumental purposes, the TVEI has been turned into something with real educational validity because the teachers who have implemented it have enjoyed a freedom of interpretation, albeit within a broad framework created by the government and maintained through the mechanism of the allocation of resources. There is also the evidence which emerged from the shift of focus of the Schools Council, in its later years, which we noted earlier, away from the production of centrally prescribed, even 'teacher-proofed', curriculum packages towards supporting school-based initiatives. School-based curriculum development and school-centred innovation – the very antithesis of the National Curriculum – have been major features of curriculum change and development during the last decade, as it has come to be appreciated with ever increasing clarity that teachers can and will implement innovations efficiently and effectively only if they themselves recognize the need for change and the value of the changes being suggested to them. Nor is this a matter of bloody-mindedness on their part; it is merely that effective education must come from the heart rather than from the head; it must be approached with conviction; it cannot ever be a mechanistic process; and this is why 'teachers make poor operatives of other people's ideas' (Simons, 1988, p. 86). It has long been apparent that evolution works in ways in which revolution never can.

There is thus not only negative evidence of the ineffectiveness of the centre–periphery approach to curriculum innovation and change; there is also positive evidence of the success of those attempts at innovation and change in which teachers themselves have been directly involved.

In part this is recognized by the planners of the National Curriculum. For we are told in the consultative document (DES, 1987, para. 67) that 'the full force of teacher professionalism will need to be put behind the national curriculum and assessment if both are to be beneficial to pupils and other "consumers" of the educational service'. This is obviously true, since neither the Secretary of State nor his DES and HMI aides can 'deliver' the goods themselves. The level of professional support needed, however, has not been appreciated, nor, more importantly, has the nature of that teacher involvement which is essential to effective implementation.

One reason for this failure to appreciate, or at least to accept, what kind of professional involvement in the planning and implementation of any curriculum is essential to its success is the fact that the kind of involvement which is required for effective implementation entails also a process of continuous curriculum development, and indeed of professional development too. Again, much research and experiential evidence points to the fact that effective education is inextricably linked not only to teacher participation in curriculum planning and innovation, but also to school-based curriculum development or school-centred innovation, and to teacher development, to notions of 'action research', 'the teacher as researcher' and 'reflective teaching' as a basis for professional development.

There are two consequences of this: first, if we want a proper and effective form of curriculum innovation or change, we must involve teachers centrally in the planning process; second, and conversely, if we do involve teachers centrally in curriculum planning, we will also get continuous curriculum development whether we want it or not. Further, this is the only route to an effective form of professional development for teachers, both collectively and individually. The concepts of action research, of the teacher as researcher and of the teacher as reflective practitioner have been shown, both theoretically and in practice, to be central to the development not only of the curriculum but also of the teacher him- or herself. What must also be recognized, and accepted, however unpalatable it may be to those whose goal is a tight centralized control, is that they are essential to effective teaching too.

As a consequence, it must be noted that the failure to involve teachers at any significant points in the planning of the National Curriculum, and the attempt to reduce their role in the educational process, must not only stunt their development as a profession and their professional growth as individuals, nor must it only inhibit the development and continued evolution of the curriculum, it must also have serious implications for the quality of what they will be able to offer their pupils. Professional expertise is a much wider concept than knowledge of subject and skill in methods of transmitting that subject to children. And it is the nature and the quality of the interaction of the teacher with all dimensions of the curriculum which will determine the quality of that curriculum as it is received by his or her pupils.

In a great many ways, then, teachers are crucial to the success of any educational development. But again one can see no recognition of this either in the framing of the National Curriculum or in the steps which have been taken towards its implementation.

SUMMARY AND CONCLUSIONS

The last two chapters have begun from the premise that any attempt at curriculum change as sweeping as that of the establishment of the National Curriculum could properly and acceptably be based only on either new preparatory research or a thorough knowledge and complete awareness of all existing research and experience in curricular and educational practice. It was claimed, therefore, that an exploration of the degree to which this is the case with the National Curriculum must be a major part of any critical evaluation of that curriculum.

Both chapters have explored a number of areas where experience and research studies have taught us many things about curriculum, about education, about children and about teachers. In Chapter 4 we considered at some length what has been learnt about assessment and its impact both on pupils and on the curriculum itself. We saw some of the problems of attaining levels of accuracy of a kind to justify the extensive programme of assessment which is currently being introduced, and suggested that the evidence available indicates that there is an inverse correlation between accuracy of assessment and sophistication of educational aims or concerns. In this chapter we have noted some of the insights which have been gained into children's minds, into how they develop intellectually, into how they respond to certain kinds of educational provision. We saw how important it is for a proper form of educational development that they be directly involved and engaged in the substance of that development. We saw, too, how they react when that substance reflects values which are not their own, and especially when it reflects values which appear to diminish their own values and to devalue their own culture, when there is a clash between the values and the view of culture implicit in the curriculum they are offered and their own values and culture. We noted that, far from leading to enhanced standards, this experience has always resulted in underachievement, especially for certain social and ethnic groups within society, and that it has, as a consequence, been a bar to the achievement of a properly egalitarian system and indeed has been a prime source of élitism.

We then considered the extent to which the planning of the National Curriculum has ignored most of what we have learned about the problems of the education of pupils with special needs, especially the experience gained since the publication of the Warnock Report (DES, 1978a) and the attempts to implement its policy of integration. We noted in particular that the lack of sophistication in the thinking behind the National Curriculum, and especially the simplistic concept of curriculum which it has adopted, were likely to lead to particularly serious difficulties in relation to those pupils whose education requires a high degree of subtlety and flexibility.

We considered next the impact of the National Curriculum on the teachers, noting all the evidence which points to the centrality of the teacher both in the education of the individual pupil and in any attempt at curriculum change or development which is to be successful. External control and direction, attempts at dissemination from the centre to the periphery, appear not to bring about real change, even though they may effect superficial changes at the surface, changes in the 'planned' or the 'official' curriculum but not in the 'real' or 'actual' curriculum which is received – or at least not changes of the kind intended or even wanted.

In all these areas we were forced to the conclusion that little or no heed has been paid to them by those planning the National Curriculum, that it is as though these lessons had never been learnt nor these messages received. In this respect too, then, the National Curriculum must be recognized as being seriously flawed.

For these lessons and messages are not merely such as to point us in the direction of a different educational philosophy or ideology. Many of them may indeed do so, but that is not the point here. That point is that they reveal also what can and what cannot be done, what is possible as well as what may be desirable. They reveal that a curriculum plan which seeks to ignore them does so at its own peril, that in many important respects it cannot work, and that in others it can do so only by accepting forms of schooling which will fall far short even of its own rhetoric. And they suggest that our maintained schools are now blessed – or cursed – with an unworkable set of procedures which are likely to lead them to disaster.

The question which must next arise is whether this must necessarily be the case with any national curriculum, whether it is the very concept of a national curriculum which is flawed or merely the amateur form of national curriculum which has been imposed upon the schools of England and Wales. This question is addressed in the next chapter.

6

THE CONCEPT OF A NATIONAL CURRICULUM

Previous chapters have set out, first, to describe the major features of the National Curriculum which has now been introduced into schools in England and Wales, second, to identify its underlying principles, its ideology, its concept of education and schooling, and third, to draw attention to many fundamental weaknesses in its structure, weaknesses of both a conceptual and an empirical kind, derived from a failure, or an unwillingness, to take account of knowledge, understanding, insights and experience available from earlier studies and previous practice.

An important question which the identification of such weaknesses raises is whether such weaknesses are inevitable, whether a national curriculum must always evince these flaws or whether they are peculiar to this national curriculum, whether there is something inherently wrong with the concept of a national curriculum or merely with this amateur attempt to turn that concept into reality.

This is the issue which this chapter will address. And it will do so by considering, first, the different kinds of reason which have been put forward, not only by politicians, but also by educational theorists from the time of Plato, for national control of education and for the provision of a common curriculum for all pupils; and, second, by considering whether there exists, or could exist, a form of national curriculum which would satisfy all or some of their demands and at the same time prove to be both a workable proposition and an educationally defensible and acceptable policy.

It is perhaps worth noting before we embark on this that the central determination of a common curriculum is the accepted practice in almost every other country, certainly in those we might describe as advanced industrial societies. In this respect, the United Kingdom has hitherto been a notable exception. There are varieties in the degree of central determination and control, and in the nature of the prescribed curriculum, and, as we saw in Chapter 4, nowhere else is there an assessment programme as extensive as that being introduced in England and Wales, but the concept remains much the same. Thus in the USSR there is a core curriculum for the ten-year school which sets out not only the range of subjects to be included for each year group but also the number of hours per week to be devoted to each, a form of requirement so precise that there is little scope left for the addition of other subjects at the discretion of the individual school. This scheme has been taken as the basic model for the curriculum in all Eastern bloc countries. Not all countries specify hourages in this way. Some leave more time for optional areas of study. There is variation in the degree of control exercised in relation to different age groups of pupils. And sometimes – as, for example, in West Germany – more than one common curriculum is established to cater for pupils deemed to be of different intellectual abilities. However, the principle of central control and determination of a high proportion of the curriculum and certainly of those subjects regarded as most important – because most useful economically and commercially – has long been well established and virtually unquestioned outside the United Kingdom. Thus the debate elsewhere has for some time centred on the nature and extent of a common national curriculum not on its desirability.

In the United Kingdom a common curriculum did not exist until the 1988 Education Reform Act made this a requirement of all schools in England and Wales. It is interesting to note the similarities of provision which were to be seen in schools throughout the United Kingdom despite their apparent freedom to devise their own curricula. This in itself may constitute an interesting contribution to the debate. However, that debate, centring as it has in this country on the desirability rather than the nature of a common national curriculum, has gone on for some time, and we must now consider its major features.

We should perhaps first note that, as John White (1988, p. 120) has pointed out, 'there is no virtue in a national curriculum as such. Hitler had a national curriculum, and so did Stalin. The basic issue is: what *kind* of national curriculum is Mr Baker giving us?' Thus the central concerns must be both the desirability of a national curriculum and the nature of any such curriculum which is proposed. And both these concerns can be satisfied only if particular proposals are placed not, as with, for example, the DES consultative document (DES, 1987), in a sea of rhetoric, but in the context of the continuing debate about both of them. Proposals for the introduction of a common curriculum for the third and fourth years of Scottish secondary schools, for example, began from a clear awareness that all curriculum design must start from fundamental principles, which are themselves, inevitably, matters of debate. What educational aims should the schools set themselves? What human capacities should they try to foster? What kinds of knowledge are of most worth? These are the perennial questions for curriculum designers; and over the years teachers, philosophers, psychologists, industrialists, educational theorists, defenders of tradition, revolutionaries and others have offered very different answers.

(Scottish Education Department, 1977, p. 15)

In contrast, one can see nowhere in the official documentation which has poured forth in support of the National Curriculum for England and Wales any reference to, any awareness of, or any attempt to contextualize its proposals within a debate which has a long history in the British educational scene.

The reasons people have put forward in support of state control of the curriculum and the provision of a common curriculum for all pupils fall into three or four broad categories, and we must consider each of these in turn. They are, first, instrumental reasons of political expediency; second, those which derive from certain views about the nature of knowledge and of culture and consequently of what knowledge an educational curriculum must include; and, third, those prompted by the desire to secure equality of educational provision for all children, regardless of class, race, gender or any other aspect of their background and origins. This last form of justification shades into what one might call the educational case, that which is based on the aim of promoting the educational development of all pupils. This educational case, however, will lead us into what is the central issue of this chapter, namely whether that aim is best achieved by commonality or difference of provision, and, if it is through commonality, what form of commonality is likely to do the trick.

THE POLITICAL CASE

The instrumental, or political, case for a common national curriculum has three broad strands to it. It justifies such a curriculum, first, as a means to economic advancement, second, as a device for maintaining a high level of social control, and, third, as the best means towards achieving the kind of centralized control of the education system which is needed to attain most effectively the first two goals. These, it will be seen, add up to a justification which is economic and political; it is not educational; it is not even a moral argument; it is a matter of political and economic expediency.

These, as we saw earlier, are the three main concerns of the new National Curriculum in England and Wales, and also of the national curricula of other major advanced industrial societies such as West Germany, Japan and the USSR. It is also worth noting that these have been the concerns of all who have advocated the use of a state-maintained education system for the benefit of the state.

For Plato, for example, for whom education was a device for bringing about the kind of society he wished to see, or felt ought to be, brought about, education was to be used certainly to ensure the economic health of society but primarily, and more important, to ensure its social cohesion and the continued control of the ruling élite. Thus, he advocated very close censorship of the kinds of music, art and literature to which pupils were to be exposed (and he wished to extend that censorship to the adult members of society too) to ensure that they would become familiar with only the 'right' values – a set of attainment targets carefully chosen to reflect the values the planners wished to impose. Included among this package of values, incidentally, was the 'magnificent myth' or the 'noble lie' we noted in Chapter 2, that all people are born with either gold or silver or bronze in their souls and that this determines their proper place and station in society.

We also noted in Chapter 2 that from the beginning of the state-maintained education system in this country a strong influence has been exercised on its development from those whom Raymond Williams (1961) called 'the industrial trainers', and that within that tradition there has always been a strong element of 'gentling the masses' (Gordon and Lawton, 1978). There are also examples of a common national curriculum being used to impose a common culture on a pluralist society – as, for example, in the USSR – and we have already noted that this is the effect and probably the intention of the National Curriculum in England and Wales. Any curriculum, as we have noted before on several occasions, will reflect the values of its authors, and, when it is the only curriculum available, will have the effect of imposing those values on all pupils. Furthermore, it is quite clear that, when the concern is also to achieve central control of the curriculum, such imposition must be the intention as well as the effect of this kind of national curriculum. It might perhaps be pointed out here that, for reasons which we noted in the last chapter, under this kind of scheme not all pupils will actually *receive* the same curriculum, since all will respond differently to it, and those whose values are at odds with those implicit in the National Curriculum may well reject it, so that, whatever is the intention, the actuality may not be a common curriculum at all. In these circumstances, the 'actual' curriculum is likely always to be rather different from the 'planned' curriculum, and the 'received' from the 'official'.

Two other aspects of this form of justification for a common curriculum are also worth noting. The first of these is that in many such cases, and certainly in the case of the National Curriculum, the case for it 'proceeds by political assertion, not the accumulation of evidence' (Barker, 1987, pp. 8–9) and by 'a ruthless slander of previous efforts rather than research and evaluation' (ibid.). The school is seen as 'a deficit system' (Holt, 1987a) and the new curriculum offered as the remedy. And, as we have seen from the last two chapters, existing research and experience are ignored and no attempt is made to obtain new data upon which to demonstrate that the new scheme is soundly based.

Second, we have also seen that no curriculum plan is ever offered with a clear statement that these kinds of political goal are its basic justification and motivation; these are never the *stated* arguments. Such political reality is always concealed behind a much more palatable rhetoric. Plato offered us the ideals of 'the philosopher king', the 'forms of knowledge' and the supreme form of 'Beauty, Truth and Goodness'. These ideals succeeded in concealing for centuries the realities of the social engineering that was at the root of his 'ideal state', his 'Republic'. And we have seen throughout this book that the realities of the new policies we have been exploring are obscured by the rhetoric of 'broad and balanced curriculum', 'entitlement', 'spiritual, moral, cultural, mental and physical development' and many other such high-sounding phrases. Indeed, there continues to be a hankering after what seem to be more acceptable forms of justification for a common national curriculum, and a recognition of the prior claims of Crowther's 'social service' and 'right of every child' view of the education system, even though the realities of what is required indicate that stark political and economic aims are the sole concerns, that the 'national investment' view is the only view and that it is this view which determines the actualities of the planning. As Denis Lawton (1988, p. 19) has said, the 'plan for a national curriculum may be accompanied by some of the common curriculum rhetoric, but does not show its ideals'.

The appeal, then, is always, at least on the surface, to other, more readily defensible, arguments, and it is these we must now consider.

THE CASE FROM THE NATURE OF KNOWLEDGE AND CULTURE

From the very beginning, discussions of education have been intimately linked to theories of knowledge. This is not unreasonable, since, whatever else education is seen to be, it must have some connection with the acquisition of knowledge – a connection which is conceptual and not merely contingent. Thus, those whose view of knowledge is that there are timeless or eternal truths, certainties, bodies of knowledge and understanding which enjoy a status derived from such certainty and timelessness, those who regard the intellect itself as a source of such knowledge and the human senses, by contrast, as a source only of uncertainty and even deception, have always regarded education as the process by which the young are offered access to these superior kinds of knowledge (Kelly, 1986).

Thus Plato, having outlined that scheme to which we referred earlier for training the citizens of his Republic to be hard-working and law-abiding artisans, proceeded to establish a further system of education for those selected as suited to it: the persons with gold in their souls. That system consisted of initiating them into what he argued was knowledge in this pure sense, a progressive course of study leading to ever greater levels of intellectual abstraction – a hierarchy of attainment targets in the profile component 'Abstract Thinking' – and to ever more independence from the uncertainties of what they might 'learn' from their senses, a course which introduced those chosen to pursue it to the 'forms of knowledge' and culminated in the appreciation of the supreme form of 'Beauty, Truth and Goodness', which encapsulated all human knowledge, aesthetic, intellectual and moral, in its fully perfected state.

Others have refined this rationalist view of knowledge over the centuries which have passed since the time of Plato, and have reaffirmed it in several different forms. Some, like Aquinas, have seen this kind of knowledge as quite literally God-given, progressively revealed by God to humankind. Others, like the German Idealists of the eighteenth and nineteenth centuries, and most notably Kant and Hegel, have attempted to set up elaborate theoretical systems to establish the same view without the embarrassment or disadvantage of the mysticism of an appeal to a deity. All have been concerned to offer a critique of knowledge which would demonstrate that some kinds of knowledge have the certainty and superiority they wished to claim for them.

More recently, as we saw in Chapter 2, this view of knowledge has been adopted as the basis for what has, during the last two decades or so, been a very influential theory of education in the United Kingdom, that theory first enunciated by Richard Peters (1965, 1966), that it is possible to identify certain 'intrinsically worthwhile activities' and that education must consist of initiating pupils into these. As for Plato, these activities are those which involve the intellect rather than the senses, the mind rather than the body, and demonstrate the highest levels of intellectual engagement.

Subsequent writers have fleshed this theory out in several ways. John White (1973), for example, has argued that these are activities which require active involvement for full appreciation, and, using that criterion, he lists them as communication, mathematics, the physical sciences, art appreciation and philosophical thought, so that these 'subjects' would constitute his compulsory common curriculum. And Paul Hirst (1965) has suggested that rationality is divided into several logically distinct forms, defined in terms of such things as differences in concepts, truth criteria and logical structure. He has offered several listings of what these distinctive forms of knowledge or understanding or rationality are, but these lists usually include such things as mathematics, the physical sciences, the human sciences, religion, history, fine arts and philosophy.

If one begins from this kind of conception of knowledge, it must follow that education is the initiation of the young into these areas of knowledge and understanding and the consequent development of their rational faculties; and the case for offering all the same educational diet rests squarely on the belief that there is only one diet which can properly be described as educational, that which consists of knowledge of this kind. (We will consider shortly the problems such a view offers for the education of those pupils who do not take to this kind of curriculum, those for whom this diet is unpalatable, those who, as we saw in Chapter 5, find it alienating.)

Thus, for Paul Hirst, education, or at least a 'liberal education', must offer access to all these forms of rationality in order to promote the development of the rational mind in all its dimensions. And, for John White, who expressly relates his view of knowledge to an argument for a common curriculum, education must require all pupils to pursue those areas of human knowledge which, in his opinion, they can never come to understand without participation in them.

We thus have a case for a common curriculum which is based on arguments of much greater depth and substance than those instrumental arguments of political and economic utility which we considered earlier, arguments which derive from a fundamental epistemology which is regarded as transcending considerations of the political here-and-now. It is also a case which, as we have seen, offers a rich source of rhetoric to those who wish to press that narrower political case but at the same time to try to cover some or all of its stark nakedness.

Terms like 'breadth' and 'balance', which, as we saw in Chapter 3, are extensively used but are almost literally meaningless in the context of a national curriculum which offers no indication of the scale on which 'breadth' is to be measured or the criteria against which 'balance' is to be judged, gain a clear meaning from this kind of epistemological base, offering, as it does, a plain statement of the view of knowledge upon which its educational prescriptions are founded. We might also note in passing that this indicates not only the extent of the rhetoric which has accompanied the implementation of current policies but also that any theory of education or act of educational planning requires a clear statement of its underlying epistemology (Kelly, 1986), since without that it lacks a secure theoretical foundation.

Allied to, indeed derived from, this kind of epistemological justification for a common curriculum is the argument, which we considered in Chapter 2, based on the claim that the curriculum should seek to transmit the culture of society and should be designed to convey what is worthwhile in that culture, what Matthew Arnold once described as 'the best that has been thought and said'. According to this view, the curriculum should contain 'a selection from the culture' (Lawton, 1975). We noted in Chapter 2 the kind of educational philosophy which this proposal reflects; we must note here that it has also been used as an argument for the establishment of a common curriculum, since it is seen by many not merely as a definition of what education is but also as implying, in a democratic society, the right of every child to be granted access to this culture. We must remind ourselves, too, that it is a view which presupposes that epistemological theory we have just considered, for its only sound basis is in the claim that 'some kinds of knowledge are superior in some meaningful way to other kinds of knowledge' (Lawton, 1975, p. 62), and that by inference some forms of culture are similarly superior. Only on those assumptions can we find a valid set of principles by which to make a selection from that culture and be confident that what we so select has some kind of timeless value.

There are many difficulties with this argument for a common curriculum. First, there are those which follow upon a rejection of its underlying epistemology (Kelly, 1986). If one does not see knowledge as having this timeless, eternal status as a body of 'truths' and certainties which are universally valid, and especially if one does not regard human values – moral, aesthetic, cultural, educational, even political – in this light, it must follow that the case for imposing any particular bodies of knowledge (and thus of values) on anyone is considerably weakened, if not totally demolished. And there is an alternative epistemology which many would see as more readily tenable in the twentieth century (in the wake, for example, of the work of Einstein and others which has revealed that even in the realms of mathematics and physical science such certainty is difficult to assert), an empiricist epistemology which suggests to us that all knowledge is tentative, hypothetical and temporary. Such a view, when applied to education, would indicate that the imposition of any knowledge on children in the confident and unquestioning way recommended by both the rationalists and the politicians is a highly questionable policy, not only because of its moral and political implications but also because it presents them with what, on this view, is an inaccurate picture of the nature of knowledge.

Second, that doubt must lead to a parallel lack of confidence in the validity of the claims that it is possible, even if not easy, to identify a common culture which can form the base of a common culture curriculum. An empiricist epistemology will deny that such a common culture can be identified, at least on rationalist grounds as enjoying some kind of timeless superiority; it will reject the notion that principles can be objectively established for the making of a selection from that culture; and it will thus reveal the idea of a common culture curriculum as little more than an attempt to establish and impose a unitary view of culture on everyone, reflecting little more than the imposition of the values of the dominant class and that attempt at social control we considered earlier as part of most political versions of common curricula (Young, 1971).

This leads us, third, to note that such a view is incompatible with the notion of a pluralist, multicultural society, unless it is accompanied by an argument to demonstrate that the other cultures to be found in society are inferior to that common culture of which the curriculum is to consist. Such of course must be the view of those who see some knowledge, and thus by inference some cultures, as superior to others. It cannot, however, be argued without that kind of epistemological base.

It is thus at this point that those who offer a third kind of justification for a common curriculum, that based on equality of opportunity or entitlement, enter the arena.

THE CASE FROM EQUALITY OF OPPORTUNITY AND ENTITLEMENT

The suggestion that there may be dangers in offering all pupils the same curriculum, especially if it is based on the notion of a common (hence the dominant) culture, and thus of imposing upon them the values of its planners, would seem to imply that we should offer a differentiated curriculum, tailored to the different needs and cultural origins of different groups of pupils. Such an argument would also seem to be reinforced by that evidence of the alienation and rejection of educational provision which, as we saw in Chapter 5, seems to result in many cases from a mismatch of values and of cultures.

However, it has also been argued that this brings with it its own dangers, primarily because, it is claimed, it limits the opportunities of certain pupils or groups of pupils in society, aggravates any social disadvantage they may be experiencing, traps them in their culture by opening up no new horizons for them, and is thus a 'curriculum for inequality' (Shipman, 1971) and/or in itself a different form of 'instruction in obedience' (White, 1968).

There thus emerges an argument for a common curriculum which is based not on any rationalist version of epistemology or on the acceptance of any concept of commonality of culture, but on the democratic principle that in a democratic society, and especially one that was, until the 1988 Act superseded that of 1944, committed to the provision of 'education for all according to age, aptitude and ability', every child should have equal access through the school curriculum to the opportunity to make his or her way in society, to make the best of his or her abilities and talents and should have equal entitlement to the same form of education as everyone else.

Again we may note that 'entitlement' is part of the rhetoric of the National Curriculum. Again too, however, we must note that it has little meaning within a framework which is essentially competitive and whose main focus is economic, or indeed in a scheme which excuses the more privileged members of society, those in public schools and city technology colleges, from participating in this 'entitlement'. Certainly, there is no evidence, as we saw in Chapter 2, that it implies a 'weak' or 'democratic' version of the equality principle as offering worthwhile opportunities to all pupils, as 'one of the social services of the welfare state' (CACE, 1959, p. 54). Again, therefore, we note the need 'to see through the rhetoric of the national curriculum. The idea [of a common curriculum] is rightly popular in the abstract, since it can be seen to help every child to get the same worthwhile education. But those parents who support this version of it might find themselves buying not liberation for their children, but imprisonment' (White, 1988, p. 122).

For it is precisely that democratic version of equality which underpins the arguments which have been mounted for a common curriculum as designed to achieve equality for all pupils. For those arguments amount essentially to the claim that all pupils should have access to the good things society has to offer and an entitlement to share in them, and not merely equal opportunity to compete in the race for social and economic advancement.

This kind of argument, even without the underpinning of a rationalist epistemology, seems *prima facie* to be indisputable, both educationally and morally.

However, it is an argument which founders on two main issues. First, there is the theoretical and moral point that any curriculum will reflect the values of its creators, and the imposition of those values on all pupils, whatever their background and origins, even in the name of equality, must be, as we saw just now, a highly questionable form of practice.

Second, there is the practical and empirical point that the actualities of attempts to offer a common curriculum framed in these terms are those responses of rejection, disaffection and alienation which we noted in Chapter 5. We saw there that this is the result in large numbers of individual cases of the attempt to impose a curriculum reflecting one set of cultural values on pupils whose background, race and/or upbringing have given them a different set of values. Thus again all pupils do not actually *receive* the same curriculum even though all may *officially* be offered it.

Some educationists have been, and some still are, quite prepared to accept the realities of this and concede that a common curriculum is not possible and that only a 'strong' or 'meritocratic' version of the equality principle can be espoused, one which says that we must give everyone the opportunity to demonstrate that they can benefit from this kind of common educational provision, to show us that they have gold in their souls, as Plato suggests, and then offer the others something that is rather less than education in the full sense – an earlier terminus in the line of attainment targets or even a different *kind* of curriculum.

Such a solution, however, will not satisfy those who argue for a common curriculum on grounds of equality of entitlement. They are thus faced with something of a dilemma, since their claim that we need to offer a common curriculum to all seems to be at odds with both certain moral principles relating to the unacceptability of value indoctrination and the actualities of the response of large numbers of pupils to that offering.

The solution to this dilemma may lie in what we might call the educational or developmental case for a common curriculum.

THE EDUCATIONAL OR DEVELOPMENTAL CASE

The Plowden Report (CACE, 1967) made a point which is highly indicative in this context, namely that equality of opportunity need not imply similarity of provision. This point was elaborated in 1980 by the Department of Education and Science (although from the perspective of its new political role, it will not be happy to be reminded of this) in a document which proclaimed that 'a common policy for the curriculum . . . cannot be a prescription for uniformity. Enabling all pupils to achieve a comparable quality of education and potentially a comparable quality of adult life is a more subtle and skilled task than taking them all through identical syllabuses or teaching them all by the same methods' (DES, 1980, p. 2). And again, 'the curriculum . . . has to be presented as more than a series of subjects and lessons in the timetable' (op. cit., p. 3).

This points us toward the notion that it is both limited and limiting to view the curriculum in terms only of its subjects and the content of those subjects, as we have asserted on more than one occasion in criticism of the National Curriculum. Further, it suggests that we will constantly run into the problems we have already identified if we conceive of, and argue for, a common curriculum in terms of its content, whether this is seen as the subjects it must contain or the selection from the culture it must include. Education, as we saw in Chapter 2, can be conceived of in more subtle terms than that, as can the curriculum; and, further, both must be so conceived if a credible and practicable version of a common curriculum is to be achieved. In short, as we saw in Chapter 2, both must be conceived in terms of processes and principles rather than in terms of subject content.

I myself argued in 1977 that the only route to the creation of a common curriculum which might be free of the problems we have delineated would be to assert what every child is entitled to not in terms of subject knowledge but in terms of kinds of experience and intellectual and other forms of development, and leave it to the professionals to interpret this general prescription for each child in relation to the individual circumstances of each child's needs. This would be a common curriculum which, as we saw in Chapter 2, Lord Joseph suggested in his criticisms of the 1988 Education Bill in the House of Lords debate, every teacher 'should have regard for' rather than one whose effect is to constrict the teachers' practice to the detriment of the proper education of large numbers of their pupils.

At the same time, in 1977, again as we saw in Chapter 2, Her Majesty's Inspectors (DES, 1977) – although again they will not thank me for reminding them of the advice they were offering when they were still free to exercise their own professional judgement – were putting forward the same kind of solution and were suggesting that a common curriculum should be constructed in terms of eight 'areas of experience'. They offered 'eight adjectives' which they believed might collectively describe a set of experiences which would add up to something most people would be prepared to describe as an education. Their advice was that we should ensure that all children should have experiences in eight broad areas: aesthetic/creative, ethical, linguistic, mathematical, physical, scientific, social/political and spiritual. To this list, as we saw earlier, was later added 'technological'.

We thus have the basis for the framing of a common curriculum in relation to the kinds and the range of experiences children are to be provided with and the principles on which the choice of the precise nature, form and content of those experiences is to be made. The aims of education are translated not into a hierarchy of objectives or into lists and bodies of subject content but into procedural principles to guide rather than to direct or even control practice. And, furthermore, we can begin to look at those aims and the principles they give rise to in their own right. We are no longer constricted by a rationalist epistemology into the assumption that to become autonomous beings all pupils must be offered the same diet of subjects, in the face of massive sociological evidence that in many cases exposure to that subject content can, and often does, have the very opposite effect.

We can thus begin to analyse what self-determination, for example, is and, especially, what kinds of process and procedure will enable us to help pupils towards its attainment. We can respond to what we have learnt from those studies of how children's minds develop, to which we referred in Chapter 5, by accepting that the task of education is to help them through the several stages of that development, to try to ensure that they do not remain fixed at an early stage, to assist them to acquire a facility within and between the several 'forms of representation' which have been posited, and, most important, that we can do this without the restrictions of common syllabuses or subject lists. For what is common to this kind of curriculum is the principles upon which it is based, not its content.

We should note, too, that this kind of common curriculum provides a better basis for intelligible concepts of 'breadth', 'balance' and other such notions. For it enables us not only to consider the curriculum as a totality, which is one of the things which the advocates of 'breadth' and 'balance' are seeking, but also to do so from the point of view of the child, from the perspective of the curriculum actually received rather than that officially planned. It offers us a concept of 'balance' and 'breadth' framed in terms of the balance and breadth of the individual child's actual experiences rather than that 'breadth' and 'balance' which it is assumed must exist when a particular range of subjects is selected for transmission. The concept of a balance of subjects is in itself meaningless; if it gains meaning, it does so from the way in which those subjects are experienced by those who study them. And it has been pointed out, with some conviction, that children's experience of a wide range of subjects can be far from broad or balanced when, as is often the case, all those subjects are presented to them and experienced by them in an identical manner – as information to be absorbed, for example, or attainment targets to be achieved. Planning the curriculum as a whole is important, but it is the whole of what is received or experienced that matters not the whole of what is planned or offered. To put it differently, this view suggests that the 'actual' or 'received' curriculum can be common only if it is not conceived in terms of subjects and their content.

Third, it is worth noting that this provides a better basis for any concept of entitlement or indeed for any attempt to implement a genuine curriculum for equality. In this connection, it is interesting to remember that the eight 'areas of experience' of the HMI document we referred to above (DES, 1977) became the basis for what was called 'the entitlement curriculum' which was the subject both of a subsequent publication (DES, 1983) and of an attempt to implement it in the secondary schools of six local authorities.

Thus, even at the official level, thinking was moving toward a conviction not only that a common curriculum was needed in order to provide genuine equality of educational opportunity for all pupils, regardless of socio-economic or ethnic background, but also to the view that the best, indeed the only, way to avoid those problems of alienation and disaffection which we saw earlier do, and must, arise when this is interpreted in terms of a common list of subjects or a common body of content to be transmitted to, and imposed upon, all, is to define that common curriculum in terms of common 'areas of experience' and common educational processes and principles, to produce a set of curriculum guidelines rather than what is in effect not so much a common curriculum as a common syllabus. This is the route towards providing equality without uniformity, a genuine equality in difference, and especially to allowing for cultural and ethnic differences, as we saw in Chapter 2, without denying equality of access and entitlement to all the benefits of education.

The attempt to implement this 'entitlement curriculum' seems to have foundered. And the main reason for this seems to have been the desire both of HMI and of the teachers in the secondary schools to translate it into their own subject specialisms. In short, the extent of the rethinking needed to plan and implement a common curriculum of this kind seems not to have been fully appreciated. It is not enough to ask *how* my subject can contribute to this kind of curriculum and to plan one's syllabuses accordingly. One needs to ask *whether* one's subject can contribute and to recognize that what it can contribute may well need to be varied according to the needs of individual pupils. It also needs to be asked whether such a curriculum can be planned meaningfully in terms of subjects in the first place. In short, as we have seen, the planning of this kind of curriculum must start with the pupils and not with the subjects.

However, both as a theory offered by HMI and as an experiment tried in practice, this approach to the creation of a common 'entitlement curriculum' has been overtaken by the implementation of the – very differently conceived – National Curriculum.

There are two main reasons why it could not survive even to exist side by side with the National Curriculum. The first of these is the problem we have just seen which relates to the subject base of the National Curriculum. As we have seen before, a subject-based curriculum is not open to the kind of interpretation and adaptation that a curriculum based on broad educational principles and 'areas of experience' necessitates. Second, a curriculum of this kind requires, and indeed depends upon, the day-to-day interpretation and professional judgement of teachers. It is not something which can be controlled to any real extent from the political centre; it does not lend itself to remote control; it recognizes the central and crucial role that, as we saw in Chapter 5, the teacher must play in any properly educational context; and, in an attempt to ensure that education in the full sense does occur, it must offer teachers the scope to play that role to the full. For this reason, it is not an acceptable form of curriculum to those for whom it is a major concern to take effective control of the curriculum away from teachers and to locate it at the political epicentre.

CURRICULUM DEVELOPMENT AND CURRICULUM THEORY

A final aspect of this debate which must be considered is the implications of these different views and versions of the notion of a common curriculum for the continued development of the curriculum and for the generation of a worthwhile body of curriculum theory, of insights and understandings to help with and to support curriculum planning. Again to the possible embarrassment of its authors, we must begin by quoting a DES document (DES, 1981, p. 1) which tells us that 'the 5–16 curriculum cannot, and should not, remain static'. In the foreword to this document, the Secretaries of State of the time, Mark Carlisle and Nicholas Edwards, tell us that 'what is taught at school should be adapted to the needs of every pupil' (op. cit., p. iii). And the document itself goes on to say: 'It is the individual schools that shape the curriculum for each pupil. Neither the Government nor the local authorities should specify in detail what the schools should teach. This is for the schools themselves to determine' (op. cit., p. 3). The implication, therefore, is that the curriculum will not remain static if teachers have the kind of scope that it is suggested here that they should have to develop, change, modify, adapt and reinterpret it, albeit within broad guidelines.

It will perhaps also be plain that (as we saw in our brief discussion of evaluation theory in Chapter 3, and of the role of teachers in Chapter 5) it is only when teachers have the freedom to make these kinds of interpretation within broad guidelines that curriculum development can occur. A common curriculum expressed in the rigid form of the National Curriculum for England and Wales must remain a static curriculum; it must remain in its ossified state, at least until the politicians decide to change it into a different kind of static, ossified curriculum; it cannot be a dynamic entity responding naturally even to 'the changing demands made by the world outside the school' (op. cit., p. 1). The only changing demands from outside the school it can respond to are those of the politicians who created it; and it can respond to them only when they so dictate – and then only slowly and ponderously, because of the monolithic nature of the assessment programme and the costs of changing it, as we also noted in Chapter 3.

The same will be true of any common curriculum framed in terms of its content, even where that content is selected by appeal to some concept of superior knowledge or a selection from the culture. Once such a common curriculum has been defined, its subject content must ossify until it is redefined. And this must be especially true if that subject content is enshrined not only in statements of syllabus but also in a rigid framework of regular assessment. Thus a common national curriculum of this kind can develop only by fits and starts, by leaps and bounds, and not by any kind of natural process of development. Every change will need to be accompanied by dissemination of what that change requires and perhaps also the thinking behind it – a long process and one known from earlier experience of the dissemination of innovation, as we saw in Chapter 5, to be not the most reliable method for effecting real change. It becomes a mechanical rather than an organic process. As Matthew Arnold once said of the Revised Code of 1862, it 'inevitably gives a mechanical turn to the school teaching . . . and must be trying to the intellectual life of the school' (quoted in Curtis, 1948, p. 264). What was needed then, he claimed, to avoid this difficulty was 'more free play . . . for the teacher' (ibid.). (One might note in passing the freedom Matthew Arnold enjoyed as an inspector to criticize government policies openly – unlike his descendants of today, not one of whom has publicly voiced the smallest of caveats about the present system.)

What is equally serious, however, is the inhibitions that this kind of scheme creates for the continued development of curriculum theory, of our understanding of the curriculum, of what can be done with it and how. Such understandings as we have, many of which have been drawn on in the earlier chapters of this book, have come from experience, and reflection on that experience, which have grown from the practice of developing curricula in a context where such development was permitted. We know what we know about the problems of dissemination, for example, because of attempts made at disseminating innovations in the past. We know what we know about different approaches to, and models of, curriculum planning and implementation, because some teachers have been able to adopt different approaches to their curricula and to their teaching. We appreciate the many complexities of curriculum evaluation because we have experience of evaluating curricula of many different kinds in many different contexts.

Thus the absence of any central determination of the school curriculum creates a climate not only for continuous development of the curriculum but also for the steady growth of knowledge and understanding of the curriculum and of the complexities of curriculum planning and development. A common curriculum framed in terms of its principles and processes, rather than its content, and depending for its implementation on the adaptation, interpretation, actualization of, and reflection upon those principles and processes by the teachers on the ground, would permit the development both of the curriculum itself and the body of theory which must underpin it if it is to be intellectually acceptable and coherent. The kind of content-based curriculum we now have in the National Curriculum will permit the continued development of neither.

In this connection it is interesting to note not merely that many of the countries which have for some time had this kind of subject-based curriculum are currently contemplating changing it for something different, something less rigid and more flexible, but also that, when they are doing so, they are often disadvantaged by the lack of theoretical insights and understandings that they need in order to change. Some Japanese educationists, for example, are currently of the view that their national curriculum is too rigid and inflexible even to meet the needs of their industrial economy, but, in seeking to change it to something freer, they lack the very theoretical perspectives which might help them to do so. The government of Singapore too, in attempting to extend the educational opportunities offered in the arts, to compensate to some extent for what has in the past been a heavy concentration on science and technology, is looking to other countries for advice on how best to do this. And Indonesia is seeking the advice of British education-ists in developing its own system because of the width of experience they have. So the examples proliferate.

Curriculum theory can grow only out of curriculum practice. And the nature and quality of that practice must, as a result, govern the nature and scope of that theory. Britain has led the world in the development of understandings in curricu-lum theory because of the scope its teachers have enjoyed in their curriculum practice. A common curriculum framed in terms of principles and processes would not take away that scope; indeed, it would demand a full exercise of it. The National Curriculum we now have, defined in terms of nothing more than its content and heavily controlled through a rigid system of assessment, most cer-tainly will.

It is thus not the concept of a common national curriculum that is at fault in the many respects we have outlined and explored; it is the actualities of the particular form of national curriculum which has been imposed on the schools of England

and Wales by the 1988 Education Reform Act. Such a form of common curriculum is indefensible in any but the starkest of utilitarian terms.

SUMMARY AND CONCLUSIONS

This chapter has addressed the question whether the unsatisfactory features of the National Curriculum which earlier chapters have identified are inevitable and necessary concomitants of any national curriculum or merely contingent to the particular form of national curriculum we now have in this country.

In order to explore this question, the chapter considered several different arguments which have been advanced for the establishment of a common curriculum and the forms of curriculum they give rise to. The political arguments were considered and it was shown that they must give rise to a curriculum which is instrumental and utilitarian in concept and designed to use the education system to promote the economic needs of society and often also to act as a device for social control. We also noted that one of its major concerns is to establish, for whatever reason, control of the curriculum by central government.

We then considered the philosophical arguments which have been offered, from the time of Plato onward, for certain kinds of educational provision based on a view of certain kinds of knowledge, and of human activity, as being inherently superior to others, and as thus justifying their inclusion in the curriculum and the imposition of them on all children. We noted, too, that this view of knowledge also underpins the claims that a common curriculum should reflect the common culture of society and that this justifies the imposition of whatever that common culture is taken to be on all pupils. It was claimed that the theory of knowledge which lies behind claims of this kind is highly problematic and that an alternative view of knowledge, which sees it as tentative and hypothetical rather than fixed and certain, does not permit one to argue for the superiority of any particular bodies of knowledge, and certainly not for any particular form of culture. It thus offers no justification for the imposition of any one common curriculum on all pupils regardless of socio-economic, ethnic or cultural background. Such a practice, it was suggested, is no more than the imposition of the values of the dominant class in society on those who are powerless to prevent it.

We next commented, however, on the dilemma raised by the fact that if, out of respect for the point just made, we offer differentiated curricula, tailored to the individual's socio-economic, ethnic or cultural needs, we run the risk of being accused of trapping pupils in their cultures and of failing to offer them equality of access to the kinds of educational experience which might help them to develop their potential to the full and to succeed in society.

This took us on to a consideration of the case for a common curriculum based on the idea of equality of educational opportunity or entitlement. We noted the strength of this argument. We also noted, however, that, whatever its strength in theory, there is massive evidence that, as we saw in Chapter 5, it does not work in practice, that pupils are more likely to reject than to accept a form of curriculum which reflects and encapsulates values alien to them. Equality and commonality in the 'planned' or the 'official' curriculum do not ensure equality and commonality in the 'received' or the 'actual' curriculum of many pupils.

This led us, therefore, to a consideration of what we called the educational or developmental argument for a common curriculum, the argument that education is the development of certain qualities of mind, of certain intellectual and other capacities, of a range of forms of representation and understanding, and that in a democratic society all pupils are entitled to be helped to travel as far down that kind of road as they are able. The important feature of this kind of common curriculum is that what is common about it is not the content selected for every pupil's educational diet but the principles and processes underlying the selection of that content, that pupils will not all receive or be offered the same subject-matter, but they will be offered and receive the same education, the same assistance in the development of their capacities to the full.

We saw that this approach had been advocated by Her Majesty's Inspectorate and that attempts had been made to implement it in some secondary schools under the name of 'the entitlement curriculum'. We also saw, however, that it is a form of common curriculum which depends totally on freedom of scope for the individual school and teacher to interpret the general guidelines it offers to meet the needs of individual pupils and groups of pupils. That, along with the inevitable preoccupation with subject specialisms, has caused it to be overtaken, and indeed overridden, by the National Curriculum whose concern is with control by central government and with a rigidly subject-based curriculum.

We finally noted that a common curriculum based on procedural principles of this kind, and open to individual interpretation by teachers, is the only kind of common curriculum which is open to continuous natural and evolutionary development and which can also be a source for the continued development of a body of curriculum theory and understanding. We concluded that both of these would be lost in a context where there is a common national curriculum framed in different terms and thus open to change only via the most laborious political processes.

Our conclusion, therefore, was that there is no reason why a common national curriculum cannot, or should not, be designed in the best interests of pupils and teachers and in such a way as to encourage continued growth and development on all fronts. It would need, however, to be designed very differently from that which we now have. Our general conclusion, then, was that the problems earlier chapters have identified with the new National Curriculum are the products of that particular curriculum and need not be regarded as being endemic to, or as implying inevitable weaknesses in, any form of common curriculum.

Throughout these discussions we were again aware of the degree to which the concepts appropriate to one kind of case have been used as rhetoric to conceal the realities of another, in particular how concepts such as 'breadth' and 'balance', which make coherent sense in the context of a common curriculum justified in terms of a rationalist view of knowledge, or a view which posits the existence of forms of knowledge and understanding, or a demand for the exposure of pupils to a range of 'areas of experience', have been used to conceal the realities of a utilitarian version of a common curriculum where they have neither sense nor meaning. This reinforces the view that perhaps the most important task in evaluating the National Curriculum is to sort out the rhetoric from the reality and to reveal its actual substance, so that a proper evaluation of that substance can be made.

This is what this book has endeavoured to do. The next and final chapter will attempt to draw some of its threads together and perhaps to offer some positive advice and guidance on how the worst of its potential effects might be minimized.

7

IN CONCLUSION

The introduction to this book made several important claims. It asserted that the National Curriculum had been designed with little reference to professional educators or teachers and thus without benefit of the 'knowledge, skills and understanding' of those whose professional concern it has been to plan educational provision and to implement the plans so made. Subsequent chapters have indicated some, though by no means all, of the aspects of that knowledge, those skills and that understanding which the amateur planning of the National Curriculum has lacked, and some of the serious flaws which, as a result, can be detected in it. We saw in Chapter 3 some of the weaknesses in its conceptual structure, its lack of clarity over many of the concepts it uses and its failure to take account of many of the theoretical understandings which recent studies of the curriculum have made available. We saw in Chapters 4 and 5 a similar disregard of much empirical evidence, the relevance of which to any kind of curriculum planning is almost self-evident.

It was claimed, too, that there are good reasons to believe that these omissions are deliberate, that they reflect not merely ignorance of such knowledge and understandings but an unwillingness to acknowledge their signficance. And we noted that at least to some extent the conceptual inadequacies we identified might be explained as a result of the use of fine-sounding rhetoric to conceal what are perhaps recognized as stark economic realities.

It would be regarded as most odd if, once the government had approved the establishment of another airport for London at, say, Maplin Sands, the Minister of Transport, along with his or her civil servants and a selection of others drawn from commerce and industry, were to take on personally the task of planning the layout of that airport and designing the airport buildings with little or no reference to the professional advice of architects. And, in the unlikely event of such a policy being adopted, we would not be surprised were the new airport to be regarded with some suspicion by the general public as well as professional architects, or, further, if at some early stage it were to collapse.

The planning and designing of an educational curriculum for all the nation's children require skills every bit as expert as those needed for the planning and designing of an airport or any public building, so that when these activities are performed by amateurs we should be prepared for disaster as much in the one field as in the other. A national curriculum, designed, as we have seen this one to have been, without the advantage of expert professional help at its most crucial points, will not perhaps collapse with the drama and public horror which accompany the collapse of a public building – for it is not lives but merely life prospects that will be lost – but collapse it must, since its planners clearly do not possess the 'knowledge, skills and understanding' to construct a curriculum which will stand up to the stresses and strains of use or implementation, nor have they taken serious counsel from those who do.

The introduction also made the claim, therefore, that these inadequacies are likely to result in an early breakdown of the National Curriculum. Again, it is hoped that subsequent chapters will have helped to substantiate that claim. The National Curriculum, and particularly its extensive programme of testing and assessment, can only work if it is interpreted in the most unsophisticated terms, if we look to it for nothing beyond a simple mechanism for the transmission of knowledge, for a linear trip through a hierarchy of objectives and for the assessment of relatively uncomplex forms of academic attainment. If we look to it for anything more than that, for the provision, or rather for the continued provision, of experiences for pupils which might reasonably be regarded as educational, we must be disappointed. For, as we have seen, its underlying concepts of education, of curriculum, of learning, of assessment, even of children and teachers are not sufficiently elaborate to be able to provide much more than a mechanism for training pupils for industry and for selecting those most suited to such training. In so far as it might be seen as a device for securing the development of 'the potential of all pupils' (DES, 1987, p. 2) or of 'their capacity to adapt and respond flexibly to a changing world' (op. cit., p. 3) or of 'ensuring that all pupils, regardless of sex, ethnic origin and geographical location, have access to broadly the same good and relevant curriculum' (op. cit., p. 4), it will prove to be inadequate. For those ambitions, as we have seen throughout this book, constitute its rhetoric not its reality. And, as we have suggested, the planners of the National Curriculum may well themselves be in breach of the 1988 Education Reform Act, since they have manifestly failed to produce a national curriculum which will satisfy these statutory requirements.

The National Curriculum must, therefore, collapse. However, it will not collapse in the sense or in the manner in which a building might collapse. Cracks will appear – are already appearing – in its edifice. As they do, however, the professionals will paste over them – not because they want to save the National Curriculum, but because they are, must be and always will be concerned primarily with the pupils, and they will want to protect them from the worst effects of its inadequacies. Sooner or later, however, everyone will appreciate what a sorry, patched-up affair it is or has become. When that stage is reached it will be important to attempt to maintain several safeguards.

First, we must endeavour to ensure that the lessons of this fiasco are learnt and that any replacement national curriculum is planned only after full consultation with professional curriculum designers and with the teachers who must implement it. This is one reason why this book has attempted to show not only why this must be so but also what kinds of 'knowledge, skills and understanding' the architects of the present National Curriculum lack and those of its replacement must ensure they possess.

Second, it must be made quite clear, when it becomes apparent that the stated ambitions and intentions of the National Curriculum are not being realized, that this is the result of inherent weaknesses and inadequacies in the policies themselves: weaknesses and inadequacies this book has sought to highlight. And at least one purpose in doing so has been to ensure that, if and when, as has been claimed, those policies fail, it will be clear that this failure is due to the policies themselves. Otherwise, the teachers will yet again be blamed. It is their presumed 'inadequacies' which have been used as the excuse for establishing a national curriculum in the first place, since the need to raise standards, however defined, could not exist unless those standards were deemed to be low, and, with little or no evidence to substantiate it, that is the claim that has been made to justify the shift of curriculum control from schools and teachers to central government. And there is no doubt that, when these new policies fail, there will be those who will want to lay the blame again at the door of the teachers. It will be important, when that happens, to be able to point to the weaknesses and inadequacies which this book has attempted to identify as evidence that the framework which has now been created for teachers has put them into a position where, without collectively becoming members of the Magic Circle, they cannot make the scheme work properly.

A further major point which follows from this is that the adverse effects on children, especially on young children, both of the National Curriculum itself, with its elaborate assessment programme, and, perhaps more importantly, of its collapse, if such is to come, must be minimized. And, if they are to be minimized, it is the teachers alone who are in a position to ensure this. There must be a policy of damage limitation and this can only be in the hands of the teachers themselves.

It would seem most appropriate, then, to conclude this book, whose main thrust has inevitably been somewhat negative, with some positive thoughts on what small scope might still exist for teachers to try to ensure that their pupils continue to gain some educational advantage and value from their time at school.

First, it is most important that we attempt to maintain the ideals which brought us into the profession in the first place, no matter what attempts are made to separate us from them and to erode them. The 1988 Act invites teachers to go beyond the National Curriculum. This is an invitation we must accept. Conversely, we must resist the very natural temptation to 'teach to the tests', to concentrate on those areas of knowledge, and, worse, those pupils, which or who are most likely to help us to achieve high scores in the SATs exercises. We must refuse the invitation to turn education into a rat-race – for ourselves as well as for our pupils. A proper professionalism requires that we decline the invitation so clearly contained in the new policies to compete with one another. For, whatever the political rhetoric claims, children can only be the losers if we resort to such commercial competitiveness over their life prospects.

Second, we must play to the full our role in the teacher-assessment element of the testing programme, whether invited to or not. And we must go beyond what that programme asks us to assess, and assess also those aspects of the educational progress of our pupils which we feel are important and significant even if, as we have seen is inevitable, these are exactly the things which fall through the cracks of the national testing system. We must develop our own forms of record-keeping and include in them our own 'attainment targets'. And we must press the results of these assessments and the professional judgements we make of our pupils on those who would disregard them. In particular, we must communicate them to parents in order to provide them with fuller information than the testing programme will offer. And, if that means drawing their attention to the complexities of education and of educational assessment, then so be it; it is only Her Majesty's Inspectors who think it is a simple matter which can be communicated in reports which 'should be simple and clear' (DES, 1989c, para. 6.4). There is no reason why we should join them in underestimating, and indeed insulting, the intelligence level of parents.

Third, we must compare the results of our teacher-assessments with those of the national testing programme and have the confidence not to concede too readily that, where they disagree, the latter must be the more accurate simply because we hear their authors claim that they have been nationally standardized. We have seen in earlier chapters that, if they do not match our own views, that may well be because they lack the sophistication to ask, or at any rate to address, the more important questions that need to be asked about a pupil's educational progress, that the very process of national standardization will have limited the extent of their complexity, and that they may well be wrong.

Fourth, we must insist on the importance of the contribution of teachers to all forms of curriculum planning and at all stages. If the National Curriculum, when it comes to be recognized as unworkable, is to be replaced by something better, that can only be achieved if there is a proper professional input to its planning at every stage. We must insist on that as the most important lesson to be learnt from our present experiences, along with the fact that Her Majesty's Inspectorate can no longer be regarded as a credible source of such professional input, not least because experience of teaching is no longer regarded as essential for appointment to it.

Finally, if we are to do all these things, we will need to develop a more substantial and rigorous base of professional theory than we have had in the past, and perhaps one way toward this is much closer collaboration between teachers in the schools and those who study educational issues in higher education. We will need to make our own evaluations of the National Curriculum as it unfolds, since, as we have seen, the official evaluations are unlikely to go far enough; we will need to make our own assessments of our pupils; and we will need to be able to defend and support both with a properly articulated form of professional understanding. For it is unlikely that anyone will do very much to support us in this. The climate, as we have seen throughout this book, is not right for the encouragement of questioning of or challenge to the prevailing and official orthodoxy; and there will be no guidance except whatever we can provide for ourselves.

If these points are accepted and acted upon, it is possible that what to some people looks like the darkest hour the education service in England and Wales has faced may be turned to advantage. A profession still in its infancy and thus an easy prey to those who have wished to steal its lollipops or throw sand in its face may be forced to develop the muscle, in the form of a proper and developing body of professional understanding, to protect itself from similar bullying tactics in the future.

And the importance of that lies not simply in what it will do for the teaching profession; it lies much more in what it will mean for the future of the nation's children.

BIBLIOGRAPHY

BOOKS AND ARTICLES

Aldrich, R. (1988) The National Curriculum: an historical perspective, in Lawton and Chitty (eds.), pp. 34–48.

Archambault, R. D. (ed.) (1965) *Philosophical Analysis and Education*, Routledge and Kegan Paul, London.

Aspin, D. (1981) Utility is not enough: the arts in the school curriculum, in White *et al.*, pp. 40–51.

Barker, B. (1987) Prevocationalism and schooling, in Holt (ed.).

Blenkin, G. M. and Kelly, A. V. (1987) *The Primary Curriculum*, 2nd edn, Paul Chapman, London.

Blenkin, G. M. and Kelly, A. V. (eds.) (1988) *Early Childhood Education: A Developmental Curriculum*, Paul Chapman, London.

Blyth, W. A. L. (1965) *English Primary Education: A Sociological Description*, Vol. II, Routledge and Kegan Paul, London.

Broadfoot, P. and Osborn, M. (1987) French lessons, *Times Educational Supplement*, 3 July.

Bruner, J. S. (1968) *Towards a Theory of Instruction*, Norton, New York.

Bruner, J. S. and Haste, H. (eds.) (1987) *Making Sense: The Child's Construction of the World*, Methuen, London and New York.

Connaughton, I. M. (1969) The validity of examinations at 16+, *Educational Research*, Vol. 11, no. 3, pp. 163–76.

Cox, C. B. and Boyson, R. (eds.) (1977) *Black Paper 1977*, Temple Smith, London.

Cox, C. B. and Dyson, A. E. (eds.) (1969a) *Fight for Education: A Black Paper*, Critical Quarterly Association, Manchester.

Cox, C. B. and Dyson, A. E. (eds.) (1969b) *Black Paper Two: The Crisis in Education*, Critical Quarterly Association, Manchester.

Crosland, A. (1961) Some thoughts on English education, *Encounter*.

Curtis, S. J. (1948) *History of Education in Great Britain*, University Tutorial Press, London.

Curtis, S. J. and Boultwood, M. E. A. (1960) *An Introductory History of English Education Since 1800*, University Tutorial Press, London.

Daniels, J. C. (1961) The effects of streaming in the primary school I. What teachers believe, *British Journal of Educational Psychology*, Vol. 31, pp. 67–78.

Denvir, B. and Brown, M. (1987) The feasibility for class-administered diagnostic assessment in primary maths., *Educational Research*, Vol. 29, no. 2.

Douglas, J. W. B. (1964) *The Home and the School*, MacGibbon and Kee, London.

Douglas, J. W. B., Ross, J. M. and Simpson, H. R. (1968) *All Our Future*, Davies, London.

Eisner, E. (1982) *Cognition and Curriculum*, Longman, London and New York.

Eisner, E. (1985) *The Art of Educational Evaluation: A Personal View*, Falmer, Lewes.

Elliott, J. (1976) Preparing teachers for classroom accountability, *Education for Teaching*, Vol. 100, pp. 49–71.

Freire, P. (1972) *Pedagogy of the Oppressed*, Penguin, Harmondsworth.

Gipps, C. (1988) What exams would mean for primary education, in Lawton and Chitty (eds.).

Goddard, D. (1985) Assessing teachers: a critical response to the government's proposals, *Journal of Evaluation in Education*, Vol. 8, pp. 35–8.

Goodson, I. (1983) *School Subjects and Curriculum Change*, Croom Helm, Beckenham.

Gordon, P. and Lawton, D. (1978) *Curriculum Change in the Nineteenth and Twentieth Centuries*, Hodder, London.

Hirst, P. H. (1965) Liberal education and the nature of knowledge, in Archambault (ed.).

Holt, M. (1987a) *Judgement, Planning and Educational Change*, Harper & Row, London.

Holt, M. (1987b) *Skills and Vocationalism: The Easy Answer*, Open University Press, Milton Keynes.

Hooper, R. (ed.) (1971) *The Curriculum: Context, Design and Development*, Oliver and Boyd in association with the Open University Press, Edinburgh.

Hoyle, E. (1969) How does the curriculum change? 2. Systems and strategies, *Journal of Curriculum Studies*, Vol. 1, pp. 230–9; also in Hooper (ed.).

Hughes, M. (1986) *Children and Number: Difficulties in Learning Mathematics*, Blackwell, Oxford.

Illich, I. (1971) *Deschooling Society*, Calder, London.

Jackson, B. (1964) *Streaming: An Education System in Miniature*, Routledge and Kegan Paul, London.

Kelly, A. V. (1977) *The Curriculum: Theory and Practice* (revised 2nd and 3rd edns in 1982 and 1989), Paul Chapman, London.

Kelly, A. V. (1986) *Knowledge and Curriculum Planning*, Paul Chapman, London.

Lawton, D. (1975) *Class, Culture and the Curriculum*, Routledge and Kegan Paul, London.

Lawton, D. (1987) Fundamentally flawed, *Times Educational Supplement*, 18 September.

Lawton, D. (1988) Ideologies of education, in Lawton and Chitty (eds.).

Lawton, D. (1989a) Culture and the National Curriculum, *Compass*, Vol. 18, no. 1, pp. 7–16.

Lawton, D. (ed.) (1989b) *The Education Reform Act: Choice and Control*, Hodder, London.

Lawton, D. and Chitty, C. (eds.) (1988) *The National Curriculum*, Bedford Way Paper 33, Institute of Education, London.

MacDonald, B. and Rudduck, J. (1971) Curriculum research and development projects: barriers to success, *British Journal of Educational Psychology*, Vol. 41, pp. 148–54.

Nuttall, D. (1989) National assessment: complacency or misinterpretation, in Lawton (ed.).

O'Connor, M. (1987) *Curriculum at the Crossroads*, an account of the SCDC national conference on Aspects of Curriculum Change, University of Leeds, September 1987, School Curriculum Development Committee, London.

Peters, R. S. (1965) Education as initiation, in Archambault (ed.).

Peters, R. S. (1966) *Ethics and Education*, Allen & Unwin, London.

Peters, R. S. (ed.) (1973) *The Philosophy of Education*, Oxford University Press.

Pilditch, J. (1987) *Winning Ways*, Harper & Row, London.

Powell, E. (1985) A modern barbarism, *Times Educational Supplement*, 4 January.

Shipman, M. D. (1971) Curriculum for inequality? in Hooper (ed.).

Simons, H. (1988) Teacher professionalism and the National Curriculum, in Lawton and Chitty (eds.).

Snow, C. P. (1959) *The Two Cultures*, Cambridge University Press, London.

Sockett, H. (1976) Teacher accountability, *Proceedings of the Philosophy of Education Society*, pp. 34–57.

Stenhouse, L. (1975) *An Introduction to Curriculum Research and Development*, Heinemann, London.

Tawney, R. H. (1921) *The Acquisitive Society*, Bell, London.

Torrance, H. (1989) Theory, practice and politics in the development of assessment, *Cambridge Journal of Education*, Vol. 19, no. 2, pp. 183–90.

Wedell, K. (1988) The National Curriculum and special educational needs, in Lawton and Chitty (eds.).

White, J. P. (1968) Education in obedience, *New Society*, 2 May.

White, J. P. (1971) The concept of curriculum evaluation, *Journal of Curriculum Studies*, Vol. 3, pp. 101–12.

White, J. P. (1973) *Towards a Compulsory Curriculum*, Routledge and Kegan Paul, London.

White, J. P. (1981) Enigmatic guidelines, in White *et. al.*, pp. 9–17.

White, J. P. (1988) An unconstitutional National Curriculum, in Lawton and Chitty (eds.).

White, J. P., Black, P., Ogborn, J., Crick, B., Hornsey, A., Aspin, D. and Lawton, D. (1981) *No, Minister: A Critique of the DES Paper The School Curriculum*, Bedford Way Paper 4, Institute of Education, London.

Williams, R. (1961) *The Long Revolution*, Chatto, London.

Young, M. F. D. (ed.) (1971) *Knowledge and Control*, Collier-Macmillan, London.

GOVERNMENT REPORTS AND OTHER OFFICIAL PUBLICATIONS

Central Advisory Council for Education (1954) *Early Leaving*, HMSO, London.

Central Advisory Council for Education (1959) *15 to 18* (the Crowther Report), HMSO, London.

Central Advisory Council for Education (1963) *Half Our Future* (the Newsom Report), HMSO, London.

Central Advisory Council for Education (1967) *Children and Their Primary Schools* (the Plowden Report), HMSO, London.

Committee on Higher Education (1963) *Higher Education* (the Robbins Report), HMSO, London.

Department of Education and Science (1977) *Curriculum 11–16*, HMSO, London.

Department of Education and Science (1978a) *Special Educational Needs* (the Warnock Report), HMSO, London.

Department of Education and Science (1978b) *The West Indian Community. Observations on the Report of the Select Committee on Race Relations and Immigration* (Cmnd 7186), HMSO, London.

Department of Education and Science (1980) *A View of the Curriculum*, HMSO, London.

Department of Education and Science (1981) *The School Curriculum*, HMSO, London.

Department of Education and Science (1983) *Curriculum 11–16: Towards a Statement of Entitlement*, HMSO, London.

✕ Department of Education and Science (1987) *The National Curriculum 5–16: A Consultation Document*, HMSO, London.

Department of Education and Science (1988a) *National Curriculum: Task Group on Assessment and Testing: A Report*, HMSO, London.

Department of Education and Science (1988b) *National Curriculum: Task Group on Assessment and Testing: Three Supplementary Reports*, HMSO, London.

Department of Education and Science (1989a) *English for Ages 5 to 16*, HMSO, London.

Department of Education and Science (1989b) *National Curriculum Design and Technology Working Group Interim Report*, HMSO, London.

Department of Education and Science (1989c) *National Curriculum: From Policy to Practice*, HMSO, London.

Department of Education and Science (1989d) *ERA: A Bulletin for School Teachers and Governors*, Issue 4, Autumn, HMSO, London.

Department of Education and Science (1989e) *The Education Reform Act 1988: The School Curriculum and Assessment*, Circular No. 5/89, HMSO, London.

Department of Education and Science (1989f) *National Curriculum History Working Group Interim Report*, HMSO, London.

Scottish Education Department Consultative Committee on the Curriculum (1977) *The Structure of the Curriculum in the Third and Fourth Years of the Scottish Secondary School*, HMSO, Edinburgh.

Secondary Schools Examinations Council (1960) *Secondary School Examinations other than the GCE* (the Beloe Report), HMSO, London.

Select Committee on Race Relations and Immigration (1977) *The West Indian Community*, Vol. I, House of Commons Report No. 180, HMSO, London.

INDEX OF NAMES

INDEX OF SUBJECTS